WITCHCRAFT FOR BEGINNERS

"A Basic Guide For Modern Witches To Find Their Own Path And Start Practicing To Learn Spells And Magic Rituals Using Esoteric And Occult Elements Like Herbs And Crystals"

BY

Diane J: Lockhart

© **Copyright 2020 Diane J: Lockhart**
All rights reserved.

This document is geared towards providing exact and reliable information about the topic and issue covered. The publication is sold with the idea that the publisher is not required to render accounting, officially permitted or otherwise qualified services. If advice is necessary, legal or professional, a practiced individual in the profession should be ordered.

From a Declaration of Principles which was accepted and approved equally by a Committee of the American Bar Association and a Committee of Publishers and Associations.

In no way is it legal to reproduce, duplicate, or transmit any part of this document in either electronic means or printed format. Recording of this publication is strictly prohibited, and any storage of this document is not allowed unless with written permission from the publisher. All rights reserved.

The information provided herein is stated to be truthful and consistent, in that any liability, in terms of inattention or otherwise, by any usage or abuse of any policies, processes, or directions contained within is the sole and utter responsibility of the recipient reader. Under no circumstances will any legal obligation or blame be held against the publisher for any reparation, damages, or monetary loss due to the information herein, either directly or indirectly.

Respective authors own all copyrights not held by the publisher.

The information herein is offered for informational purposes solely and is universal as so. The presentation of the information is without a contract or any guarantee assurance.

The trademarks that are used are without any consent, and the publication of the logo is without permission or backing by the trademark owner. All trademarks and brands within this book are for clarifying purposes only and are owned by the owners themselves, not affiliated with this document

Table of Contents

INTRODUCTION 1

History of Witches 3

WHAT IS WITCHCRAFT? 7

TYPES OF WITCHES 11

WHAT IS THE MARK OF A WITCH? 19

WHAT DOES IT MEAN TO PRACTICE WITCHCRAFT? 22

HOW TO PRACTICE WITCHCRAFT 26

    Spells of Magic and Witchcraft for Beginners 29

    Witchcraft for Beginners: 10 Tips on How to Start the Right Way ... 32

    Techniques for Training Your Mind 37

    Essential Skills for the Beginner Witch 40

WITCHCRAFT MISTAKES BEGINNERS ALWAYS MAKE 44

FIRST STEPS TO BECOMING A WITCH: ADVICE FOR BEGINNER WITCHES 51

How to Connect with Ancestors..56

A DEBUNKING OF COMMON MISCONCEPTIONS ABOUT WITCHCRAFT AS IT IS PRACTICED TODAY 58

CORE BELIEFS AND PRACTICES FOUND AMONG A VARIETY OF FORMS OF THE CRAFT 67

CLEAR DISTINCTIONS BETWEEN WICCAN, TRADITIONAL, AND ECLECTIC PATHS 84

Differences 90

Reclaiming 95

ECLECTIC WITCHCRAFT 96

Reasons for Using the Term Eclectic 98

CORE CONCEPTS UNDERLYING THE "WHY" AND "HOW" OF MAGIC 101

Ten Benefits of Learning Magic 104

TOP TEN TIPS ON HOW TO START THE RIGHT WAY 126

A BRIEF LOOK AT A FEW COMMON MAGICAL TECHNIQUES—VISUALIZATION, INVOCATION, AND CANDLE MAGIC **134**

    Black Box Technique 138

    INVOCATION AND THE PROCESS OF MAGIC 139

WITCHCRAFT SPELLS AND RITUALS **148**

CONCLUSION **150**

INTRODUCTION

Witchcraft is a craft that is commonly mistaken. In ancient times, the witches are suspected of all kinds of devilish and disgraceful deeds that seem to send thousands of people into fires of imagination as villains. It became common in the 20th century and is usually responsible for dangerous property and persons. In comparison to the recognized fly-brooming carriage for witches, a common confusion of magic as satanic rites and rituals seems to be created by the general public. It's thought that it is the activity of mystical and spiritual powers to manipulate a person, location, occurrence, or property in a good or bad way. Anthropological, theological, and social backgrounds are said to occur. It is generally perceived by the population as "evil" or "grim," probably due to the fact that the various mysterious events that took place during the 20th century are largely to blame. Basically, witchcraft is simply the magic of nature, and there's nothing wrong with learning how to witchcraft, so long as you intend to use witchcraft for personal reasons.

Witchcraft often shines and confuses certain people today, even though it's been around from the dawn of the world. And its elusiveness and

Diane J: Lockhart

mystery are probably what attracts so much curiosity. So we're learning a little about it here.

History of Witches

Early Christians in Europe regarded Witches as evil beings, creating the famous Halloween image.

Pictures of witches have appeared across centuries, from dark, wart-nosed people huddling over boiling chalk to hag-faced, shaggy creatures flying through the skies on brooms with pointed caps. The witch was portrayed in pop culture as a benevolent, nose-twitching housewife, an awkward teenager who learns her power, and three-way charmed sisters fighting the forces of evil. Nevertheless, the real history of witchcraft is grim and often dangerous for witches.

The Origin of Witches

Early witches were people who practiced witchcraft, used spells, and called on spirits to support or alter. Most witches were believed to be heathen doing the work of the devil. Many of them, though, were just natural healers or so-called' good folk' who did not understand the preference of their occupation.

It is uncertain exactly when witches arrived in historical scene, but in the Bible, in the book of 1 Samuel one of the first accounts of a witch was published in 931 B.C. And 721 B.C. And 721 This tells the story of King Saul finding the witch from Endor to carry in the spirit of Samuel, the deceased prophet, in order to defeat the Philistine army.

Samuel was shocked by the witch, who then prophesied the demise of Saul and his son. The next day Saul's sons died in battle according to the Scriptures, and Saul committed suicide.

Certain parts of the Old Testament forbid witchcraft, like the frequently quoted Exodus 22:18, stating, "You shall not let a witch live." Other Biblical references are warning about divinity, praying, or the use of witches to reach the deceased.

'Malleus Maleficarum'

In the mid-1400s, witch-hysteria took hold during Europe when many suspected witches admitted to a variety of bad actions, often under coercion. In a century, witch hunts were widespread, and most of the accused were burnt or hanged. Single women, widows, and other women were particularly targeted on the margins of society.

Around 1500 to 1660, up to 80,000 alleged witches were executed in Europe. Around 80% of them were women who are considered to be in cahoots with the devil and lustful. Britain had the highest rate of witchcraft, while Ireland had the lowest rate of adoption.

The publishing of "Malleus Maleficarum" — published in 1486 by two esteemed German Dominicans— was possibly an invitation for the witch to become viral. The novel, usually called the "Hammer of Witches," was basically a guide to how witches are found, chased, and challenged.

"Malleus Maleficarum" classified witchcraft as blasphemy and became the source of Protestant and Catholic witches rapidly. The book sold more copies of any book in Europe than the Bible for more than 100 years.

Salem Witch Trials

As the panic of the witch in Europe declined, it rose in the New World, a conflict between France and the British, a smallpox outbreak, and the continuing threat of assaults by rival American tribes. The mood became strained and eager to pursue scapegoats. Probably the most famous witch trials were held in 1692 in Salem, Massachusetts.

Salem's witch trials started after nine-youth Elizabeth Parris and eleven-year-old Abigail Williams began to suffer seizures, corporal hallucinations, and excessive crying (today an infection that triggered spasms and visions is believed to kill them). More young women began showing signs, culminating in mass hysteria, and three women were arrested with witchcraft: Sarah Fine, Sarah Osborn, and Tituba, Parris's father's pregnant aunt. Tituba confirmed that he was a witch and started accusing others of using black magic. On 10 June, when it was hanged in the Salem gallows, Bridget Bishop was the first convicted witch to be put to death during the Salem Witch Trials. As a result, about 150 men were charged, and 18 executed. Six men were also convicted and executed, not only were women victims of the Salem Witch Procedures.

However, Massachusetts was not the first of the 13 colonies to deal with witchcraft. Alse Young was the first person to be executed for witchcraft in America in 1647 in Windsor, Connecticut. Before the last witch trial took place in Connecticut in 1697, 46 men were accused of witchcraft, and 11 were executed.

Citizens were less worried about witchcraft in Virginia. In addition, in 1655, a law was passed in Lower Norfolk County that rendered it a felony to wrongfully suspect someone of witchcraft. Witchcraft was still a problem. About 1626 and 1730, over two dozen witch trials (mostly women) were conducted in Virginia. None of the suspects have been sentenced.

WHAT IS WITCHCRAFT?

The term "witchcraft" may, in reality, apply to a broad range of beliefs, customs, and rituals found in cultures around the world and since the dawn of humanity in every era of history.

It is believed that in the religion in witchcraft, certain individuals have an evil force that can cause illness and misfortune. The power should be immediately allowed, sometimes without the witch's conscious knowledge.

The heathen faith is Witchcraft. Pagan religions serve multiple myths than one deity. Paganism is one of the oldest religions which includes not only Christian, Muslim, or Jewish religions but also the Hindu, Buddhist, Taoist, Confucian, and American Indian religions as well. Paganism accounts for 50 percent of all sects, according to the 1998 Cambridge FactFinder.

The expression "pagan" is actually derived from the Latin Pagini and Pagani, terms that are considered "hearth," or "dweller's house" or, more literally, "farm guy." It wasn't until the 1450s that fear of witchcraft grew, and people started associating witchcraft and paganism with worship of the devil, evil hexes, and spells.

Of reality, the words "witch" and "witchcraft" had only terrible associations a few centuries ago. This was attributed to the need of the Christian Church for full control over the continent of Europe. Anyone who had the confidence or believed in activities outside the limits of the church doctrine was said to be operating with the "Devil" and to be "a witch." Gardner and others resurrected the "W" term to regain the religious freedoms that the Church had stripped away for so long. Most practitioners in the profession are now capitalizing on Witch and Witchcraft to differentiate their activities from scientific jargon and myths from past history.

WITCHCRAFT: A BIG UMBRELLA

Those who know Witchcraft's bigger world believe that Wicca is one of the crafts, which in effect, is a form of modern paganism. In other terms, "Witchcraft" is a parachute concept that Wicca shares with much other witchcraft. Some may have beliefs and practices that resemble contrast Wicca, while others are entirely different.

For instance, the feri culture, an art style American established by Victor and Cora Anderson in the 1930s and 40s, has its origins in both Western and East Vodou practice and occult philosophy. Stregheria is an Italian-American type of witchcraft, which derives from centuries-old practice among Italian immigrants, and was not recognized until the later twentieth century outside these groups. A more recent tradition became known as Sabbatic Craft, which draws from, among other influences, both ceremonial magic and English traditional folk magic.

In addition to these widely recognized Witchcraft practices, there are several ways of different people who practice what we could term "eclectic" craft. These can involve folk traditions from specific regions, such as Ireland and England, which endured the alleged abolition of pre-Christian rituals by the Church. Others appear to have adopted art traditions in older communities that have been passed on through centuries-long before Wicca and other manifestations of witchcraft from the 20th century. Such heritage practices tend not to stop in books or pages related to the art, as they are common and usually quiet.

Are Witches Real?

Grace Sherwood is one of the most famous witches in the history of Virginia, whose neighbors reportedly killed their pigs and hexed their cotton. There were other charges, and in 1706 Sherwood was brought to trial.

The Court decided to use a disputed water test to define its culpability or innocence. The arms and legs of Sherwood were bound and plunged into a body of water. It was believed she was innocent because she sank; she was guilty as she rose. Sherwood did not sink low and was told that he was a witch. She hasn't been murdered yet put in jail for eight years.

A humorous essay about a New Jersey Witch Trial (allegedly composed by Benjamin Franklin) was reported in the Pennsylvania Gazette in 1730. This exposed the mockery of some allegations of witchcraft. It wasn't long before the witch mania was extinguished in the New World, and legislation was passed to discourage false charges and prosecutions.

TYPES OF WITCHES

There may be unique descriptions and myths that come to mind as we hear about witches. When you think of witchcraft and the people who practice this every day, the evil queen from Snow White, Nancy from The Craft, or just a female driver on a broomstick that pops into your mind.

But there are so many actual witches, unlike what superstition and pop culture would take you to. The universe of Paganism, Neopaganism, Wicca is wide and large, and the witches are all uniquely different.

The witch has been highly recognizable— and highly stereotyped — figure in the American mentality over the decades of pop-cultural assimilation. The scowling, green-skinned elderly woman who uses hexes to kill lovely young girls and all who test it, and the calm, a relatively ordinary witch who uses her abilities mostly for good, such as the Sabrina of Bewitched (the Teenage Witch) or Samantha of Bewitched.

At the same moment, the American witch has been remembered for its tragic history–not only for its dramatic stories–due to U.S. history classes and historical fiction. The most famous in Salem were the witch hunts and trials of the late 17th century in Massachusetts, which reflected the hysteria of mass and misogyny brought about by religious fervor and paranoia.

But America isn't the only location that comes along with something evil. Women were both celebrated and punished across time and space for their alleged magical powers.

Below are descriptions of the various types of witches that one may be created and some of the truth behind what separates everyone in the witchcraft community—different types of magical beings with their own values, skills, and practices— not including broomsticks.

1. Traditional Witch

Traditional witches are witches who have a background in witchcraft tradition and the Old Craft that comes before Wicca. You take a theoretical (traditional) view to your work and often research your ancestors or other witchcraft-oriented legends. Traditional witches want to respect the "traditional" ways of their art and often concentrate on working with the local past and the spirits from where they come. While these witches have high regard for ancient history and traditions, they are entirely modern conventional witches.

2. Gardnerian Witch

The Gardnerian Wicca is a Wicca tradition that began in the 1950s and spread all over the world, thanks to Gerald Gardner, frequently called the "Father of Wicca." Gardnerian Wicca practitioners have strong relationships with nature, contradict societal standards, and have many practices that underlie their activity. To be a Gardnerian witch, members can not initiate themselves. You must be initiated. There is also an incredibly organized witch advancing method, as you grow and learn more about your art.

3. Alexandrian Witch

Alexandrian Wicca was created by Alex and Maxine Sanders in the 1960s and is a British witchcraft variant of Wicca. Alexandrian Wicca has many parallels with his sister Gardnerian Wicca, but she also incorporates ritual spells and Qabalah components. Alexandrian Wicca is more diverse than Gardnerian Wicca and less formal. You embrace the assumption that "if it works, uses it." In practice, witches must still be enrolled, and there are classes and rates of improvement that can be achieved if a witch advances with the exercise. Their covens occur during new moons, full moons, and Sabbath holidays.

4. Correllian Witch

Correllian-Nativist Tradition, or Correllian Wicca, was established by Caroline High Correll in the late twentieth century. She appeared to be a genetic witch and was an intellectual, metaphysical, and herbalist healer. She remained strongly influenced by her supposed heritage and Arabian witchcraft until her death in the 1940s. Until the 1990s, Correllian Wicca was not known as Wicca but rather as universalism. Correllian Wicca is one of the most common practices today.

5. Sea Witch

A witch of the sea has strong ties to the shore and the ocean and often incorporates this in her work. The magic of sea and ocean also includes coral, eggs, driftwood, or other items from there. Sea witches feel connected with sirens and ancient legends etc.

6. Kitchen Witch

Kitchen witches are also sometimes called a hearth witch or a house witch, and most of their magic is produced at home or in the kitchen. They are very home-based, always amazingly nourishing, and they love making their home a special and holy spot. Kitchen witches like to roast and grow plants from their own garden. In action, they incorporate their own personal and individual mystical energy to create their charms, ceremonies, and magic-using essential oils, spices, food, and other everyday items.

7. Hedge Witch

Hedge witches do the so-called "hedge hopping" that moves from this universe into the Other one. Witches will interact and send messages between the two realms with the spiritual world. Hedge witches perform astral vision and work using plants and the magic of the world. But what makes them a hedge witch specifically is their ability to cross the "hedge," also known as the frontier between this world and the spirit world. The "driving on a bumper" story was believed to be a confusion focused on hedge witches "walking" in the spiritual realm.

8. Dianic Witch

Dianic witches practice the most feminist practices of all witchcraft. Diana cult followers are all people, so no men are allowed. Through all three ways, Dianic witches honor the goddess — Maiden, Daughter, and Crone. Rituals and worship can differ, but they are all religious and are progressive.

9. Elemental Witch

Elemental witches learn and work of four elements: ground, sun, wind, and fire. Elemental magic is research on which each element is centered and honored. For each particular element, an elementary witch may have an altar. Elementary witches evoke elements while making spells and doing ceremonies, and they can even consider an element with which they mark themselves and function.

10. Ceremonial Witch

Ceremonial witches have many practices, but ceremonies and rites are highly regarded activities. Ceremonial magic is used in most of its functional aspects. You probably work a rite or custom in anything you cast or attempt to do. Ceremonial witches also invite other spirits and supernatural powers to aid them with whatever they create.

11. Green Witch

Often named garden witches or woodland witches, green witches have high energy links to the world. We may have its own greenhouse, but also research the region and experiment with local plants and its own climate. Green witches in their potions and magic using plants/greenery and sometimes also boiling them and in their kitchens. Green witches are often very natural and enjoy animals, herbs, fruit, flowers, and much more. We do this to be as close as possible to Mother Earth and the energy it holds.

12. Hereditary Witch

The hereditary witch is a witch born with bruises. This belongs to their relatives and/or sides. Their power and experience are inherited from previous generations, even if they can operate with their own specific rituals or in lieu of their relatives. There is still an option, though. Inherited witches have to be raised in fruitfulness, so you won't be inherited witches if you don't choose to perform the witchcraft.

13. Cosmic Witch

Cosmic witches are modern witches, who reach into the stars, astrology, and science and practice certain elements and cosmic powers. Such witches sometimes called "Sky Witches," observe the planets and the orientation of the stars often and focus their spells and practices on the various places.

14. Secular Witch

Secular witches also cast spells, using stones, spices, oils, and candles, but do not spiritualize. Secular witches do not worship a god or a greater creature— their custom is not entirely religious. We don't trust in solar resources or money in their jobs. This is not to suggest a secular witch can't be pagan, but just their work can't be spiritual. Both are completely separate.

15. Solitary Witch

A solitary witch may be any kind of witch, but rather than a coven, they choose to work by themselves. This could be by default, or because a party has not yet been found to work with. There are also stories that lost witches are reincarnations of sorcerers who work for centuries, and their awareness is awoken at puberty. Because they know and appreciate the craft, they have less need of a coven than a new witch.

16. Eclectic Witch

An eclectic witch has no single religion, practice, tradition, or culture. Their practice stems from many sources and ultimately becomes one of the sorcerers. We may follow a greater deity, or their religion may mainly be pagan, or they may be their own divine type. In the end, an eccentric wizard makes his own "laws"–based on the individual witch, it is entirely unique.

WHAT IS THE MARK OF A WITCH?

Witches ' marks–ceremonial indications of security or apostrophic signs–have been identified in many historic places, from medieval churches and houses to barns and caves.

The term "apotropaic" is taken from the Greek word meaning bad avoidance. The marks were typically written on stone or woodwork near the entrance points of the house, particularly the doors, windows, and fireplaces, to protect people and visitors from witches and the evil spirit.

They date from periods before witches, and the occult was generally believed. Magical symbols and ritual objects were common in life between the 16th and the early 19th centuries.

Nevertheless, their definition as a symbol for ceremonial defense is probably the most widely accepted hypothesis. They are commonly used in the form of graffiti in churches and sometimes in the designs of portable and not so mobile medieval houses, e.g., chests and heavy-stone fonts, to name just two.

In various forms of witchcraft and the practice of witchcraft, the witch symbol emerges.

The different types of witch marks are:

- A mark on the body of the witch
- A protuberance like a mass or a teat
- Devil's mark
- A symbol or a sign to prevent witchcraft.

We'll look at the different witch signs, what they represented, and why they happened.

A common type of apostrophic mark is defined as a daisy wheel, although most literature in this area identifies the marks as hexafoils.

These' bean' patterns of six lobes vary greatly in scale. According to the public answers, the hexafoil was the most common mark by far. They are definitely the simplest to recognize.

The symbol's origins can be traced back to ancient times. We were located in the early medieval English houses up to the 19th century.

The function of hexafoils is contentious. The culture of Wicca, for example, which is a new mystic religious movement, recognizes them as sun motivations. Another school of thought indicates that the training exercises are strictly philosophical and abstract-they certainly appear as math drills or in textbooks. Nevertheless, their definition as a symbol for ceremonial defense is probably the most widely accepted hypothesis. We are seen widely on churches in the form of graffiti and sometimes also on lightweight medieval items, such as chests and heavy stone font, to name but two.

They were also contained in barns used once to store grain, often around the door openings. These features on the stonework of some of the biggest barns, such as the Bradford barn on Avon, the Wiltshire barn of the 15th century, and the Middle Littleton barn doorway at Worcestershire (a National Trust property).

In many wooden structures throughout the world, hexafoils are found around barns; however, many of the responses we had to our demand for samples from all over England came from historic houses.

Some examples were provided of daisy wheels dating back to the 17th to the 19th centuries on furniture where their importance becomes more difficult to interpret: is the hexagon on a piece of furniture a ceremonial object or merely a decorative mark? This is a concern that further work will support.

What Is a Witch's Teat?

The idea that people were looking for help from supernatural beings was still there. Witches had "familiarize." Such forces had to be preserved, and witches had an additional, secret nipple that fed the family milk. According to witch-finders, every elevated lump, bump, or skin tag could be a teat.

WHAT DOES IT MEAN TO PRACTICE WITCHCRAFT?

Even if you think you are certain that you want to continue, it is best to find out what you are signing up for. When going through spell books, it's prudent to do your homework, particularly as a combination of legends and actual historical documents are mixed with the current notion of witchcraft, allowing each one to take a slightly different view of the subject. Back at the first step of knowing the risks, a valuable introduction to a witch-related past (and tragedy) of the 1600s by Katherine Howe, a seed of some of Salem's suspected witches. (Stewart's What Witches Do informs us of his history as a witch and member of a partnership formed by Alex and Maxine Sanders who co-founded Alexander Wicca in the 1960s, for a first hand— and certainly lighter— read.) If so, start with the basics (and thank your deity of choice after the advent of Google for this decision). Lisa Chamberlain has become a source for those who are interested in Wicca; her book "Wicca for beginners" basically is "Wicca 101," and there are many more books that come from both Chamberlain and her recommended reading list. If you are involved in other spirituality and/or you are up for a deeper dive, pick up Drawing Down the Moon:

witches, druids, worshipers of Goddess, and others in America Today by the late writer and priestess Margot Adler of Wiccan. The first analysis of modern paganism in the United States has persisted since its first publishing in 1979, thanks in part to its three most recent editions.

Stock up.

Depending on the type of witchcraft which you choose to pursue, at least a few supplies from an occult store, such as candles, oils, roots, and ritual herbs, spell books, tarot cards, potion ingredients, calcium cans, and a crystal ball, will probably be required for psychism-drawn ones. (Some products don't have to be purchased — for starters, the so-called Feces Spell is definitely the top of that category.)

Practice, practice, practice.

Anyways to start by learning how to dress a candle, follow any simple procedures, and familiarize yourself with the various uses of crystals and candles — all of which are documented in your Book of Shadows.

Find your coven.

First of all, brace for patience; covens may seem daunting to prevail all over the world, even in Arkansas, but their numerical power ultimately helps prevent you from being compelled by oaths in a coven into which you really are not bound. There are almost 80 covens, for example, in the New York metropolitan area, not to mention the chance to participate in the Pagan Pride Day annual festival. If you'd rather (and you could) afford to make your witchcraft, say, the comfort of pasta macaroni and grapefruit-and-cucumber-scented candles, you might want to meet a bunch of rather popular rich children whose practices the New York Times has described as "more Beyoncé than Sit-y."

Fret not if you're at a lonely and quiet side: the Internet has streamlined witchcraft through videos, tweets, and understandable lists via Instagram's newly found, thriving witch groups, many of which provide supernatural advice and consultations with support. Which of the so-called "# witchesofinstagrams" would you believe, a word of advice: despite extensive research, posing for gothic picture shots and/or esthetically appealing photographs of crystals aren't really rituals — at least yet.

Magic isn't immediate

Witchcraft does not establish the same effect, which can be dangerous results as portrayed in the films. All can and will burn if not properly, creating negative energy and drawing evil entities, including spirits.

Many people also seem to forget that spells and spells have no immediate tangible effects. Witchcraft is the use of energies to build changes in your spells. They were making love; a charm won't guarantee that they fall in love. This will help both people better communicate, care more regularly about one another, or maybe strengthen the relationship, but it will not make them both lovers. It can give them an idea, but the citizens have to act on it.

Many people, especially beginners, do not know that interacting with spirits (talking with spirits, communicating with spiritual friends) is very similar to witchcraft. They interact with nature, and both have common foundations (meditation, modulation of light, astral materials, etc.). Of course, this doesn't mean that the witch has to learn supernatural stuff, but it can allow you to connect with the spirits, especially if you need astral artifacts such as dragon scales, bats blood, and others. And basic things, such as hair. You can get an astral one if you can't get it in the physical world. This does the same thing.

HOW TO PRACTICE WITCHCRAFT

The best and easiest way to start witchcraft and make your first spell is to learn. Learn about the various traditions as much as you can and find the correspondences that are most attractive to you (physical symbols of unseen qualities or forces). You will execute a very powerful ritual without ever spending a dime. Go to your favorite spot of nature like a beach or woods to gather shells, hats, leaves, flowers, and other things that are important to you. Such items cost nothing and are as efficient as expensive electronic correspondences. In the end, it comes down to personal choice, so you should try to figure out what works best for you.

What Do I Need to Cast a Spell?

Tools or correspondences are powerful books to draw attention to and symbolize power within and in nature, but before you start witchcraft, you don't need to go out and buy some stuff. Some materials (such as flowers and herbs) can be purchased very easily or even free of charge. Some people actually argue that natural or handmade materials are better than store supplies. Below is a list of some of the most popular, both free and other witchcraft supplies and equipment.

Common Witchcraft Supplies and Spell craft Tools

- ✓ Cauldron: This little bowl, usually made of cast iron, is used for spelling mixing and heat potions. It is one of the most common healing tools available.
- ✓ Mortar and Pestle: this small cup, typically made of cast iron, is combined with a stubborn grinding tool used for the crushing of herbs and spices.
- ✓ Herbs: Different herbs are used to give benefit to medicines and potions. Sage is one of the most popular spells herbs and is used for purification and protection.
- ✓ People: Most people warrant the use of flowers for their clear symbolism and exquisite fragrances.
- ✓ Gemstones: Each gemstone has magical value and can be used as a ceremonial match or as a way of healing. Often they are used for defense, emphasis, and spelling.
- ✓ Crystals: The crystals are used typically to purify a sacred space before the ceremony, to restore and protect, and to intensify the mystical qualities of gemstones.
- ✓ Magic Amulets and Talismans: These are important objects, which can be used for the everyday protection and improvement of spell crafts or used.
- ✓ Wand: This wooden stick or other tool is used for spinning a circle.

- ✓ Athame: This sword is used to cast a magic defense circle and is used in rituals as well.
- ✓ Salt: Used widely to form a protective circle, salt prohibits evil spirits from entering a room and is used to clean up and cleanse certain protection spells.
- ✓ Statues of God and Goddess: they are used during rituals to draw attention to God and Goddess and to call their presence to a ritual circle.

While all of these items can be used as critical spell correspondences, you do not need a physical item to spell it. Witchcraft draws its influence from the wishes of the user and the magic within the human. If you can use magic, you can do this with or without these instruments.

Understanding the Principles of Witchcraft for Beginners

There are a variety of rules of Witchcraft that must be known to all beginners. Start by learning the essentials: from the witch's pyramid to training the mind to understand how to use power.

Witchcraft Primer

Primers from Witchcraft are perfect for those who want to study Witchcraft, magic, and spelling. Here's a rundown of what you need to remember and what to do. Witchcraft allows you to familiarize yourself with devices, methods, and spell components to accomplish your intentions.

Training the Mind

If you want to learn Witchcraft, preparing the mind is important. You don't have to run out of a spellbook to find an altar full of tools. What you really need to continue is to practice your mind. Once you have learned to control the mind by meditating, you can go on with techniques like imagination.

The Witch's Pyramid

The pyramid of Witch is a basic philosophy that helps to learn the craft. For all beginner witches, this is an important lesson. It is given other names such as 4 Magus Powers and 4 Sphinx and Hermetic Quarter Secrets. You can use your intelligence and imagination by learning the theory of the Witch's ladder.

Spells of Magic and Witchcraft for Beginners

Most novices are going to ask Witches for actual spells— as if they believe we're all good Witches. We're not! We're not! I guarantee that. I promise. Here's the question, when you're not learning brass music, looking for spells is like looking for playing sheets when you haven't learned how to play an instrument yet.

Sadly, you can just get other websites— many of which are from people who haven't learned crafts from reputable sources, so these spells sound like something from Charmed. But to tell a rhyme and light the fire doesn't make things "poof" and many people, therefore, have the following questions:

- ✓ Can anyone become a Witch?
- ✓ What is the first step to becoming a Witch?
- ✓ Do I need a mentor to learn Witchcraft?
- ✓ Can I be a "good" Witch?

Advice for New Witches

As a new witch, you have a lot to learn. By choosing a mentor to learn essential tools, you will start your journey in the right direction.

Choosing a Mentor or Teacher

Choosing a mentor or instructor is a significant step in learning skills. Be conscious, though, that many people do not want to be what they are. Careful selection is of utmost importance. Remember, just "doing well" with your energy work and being vigilant of those who are going to harm other men. Here are a few attributes to expect in someone who wants to become a counselor or a tutor.

Creating Channels

It is necessary to create networks by increasing energy and steering it to your target if you want to work your spells. You can't just throw them and expect things to come out of the air. You have to create channels for them. Figure out what a platform is and how to do it.

Casting Effective Spells

Some spells work, and other spells don't – you know something when you research witchcraft. So, are you looking for more ways to spell a change? Perhaps your capabilities are not the problem, they are your goals. Know through spells you don't spend your time casting.

Common Beginner Mistakes

Beginner mistakes are normal, and even the best of us have undoubtedly stumbling on at least one or two common mistakes at the outset, no matter how experienced, Therefore, forewarned is forearmed for all of you beginners out there! Sometimes it can be half the battle to learn what traps to prevent. Here are another seven beginner Witch errors.

Diane J: Lockhart

Witchcraft for Beginners: 10 Tips on How to Start the Right Way

Intention is Key

The goal is at the heart of all. This is something you really need to learn before you do any magic. Actually, witchcraft is subject to the law of attraction.

This is precisely how witchcraft and magic work. In nature, the shift you want to happen in the World is your purpose. But it's only the first step to decide. Then, with all your body cells, you have to know that purpose. Visualize the fulfillment of your desires. How does that feel? How does it smell and taste? Then put it on paper when it's solid enough. Be very careful about your sentence. If your purpose is to succeed, it must be a single sentence, using only the present tense in the first person. You should also use only positive words. Avoid using "not" or any other negative types of verbal. An example of a decent statement of intent is "I'm confident and strong." You can do whatever spell you want when you have learned your statement of intent. But remember that with all your heart, you really need to believe. If you don't, why do you first do that? To sum up, I would suggest that the purpose is motivation, language, and mere willpower. That idea was founded on all forms of witchcraft.

Follow Your Intuition Before Anything Else

I think it's worth thinking about it again, though. Witchcraft is accompanied by intention and intuition. Ask yourself while trying a new spell or ritual:« does it feel right»? Close your eyes and feel your encouragement within. If it feels right, continue. If you have a bad feeling, quit what you're doing immediately. Reflect how the spell (or ritual) can be modified to make it feel right for you. Then carry on feeling like it. This is very necessary because your spell won't work if you don't sense it. If you want, your intuition strengthened.

Be Aware of the Three-Fold Law and of the Wiccan Rede

The Three-Fold Law works on the same principle that I described previously as the Law of Attraction. Garbage in, garbage out. Joy brings joy, and vengeance brings only more wraths. The distinction is that this rule is witchcraft-specific. Since we operate at a strong level of magic, the results of what we put out are typically amplified.

This law comes from the Book of the Law by Aleister Crowley. Unlike the Three-fold statute, this provision does not address magic concepts. The Wiccan speech, in fact, is more like a general moral guideline. It is, in essence, somewhat similar to the Golden Rule found in all faiths. This says that you should treat others as you want to be treated. Even if witchcraft is not a religion, I believe it is important to follow a code of ethics. It often distinguishes between practitioners and wants tobes and charlatans. Of course, as I said before, you can cast curses and hexes, but you can't always do that. Magic is a benevolent instrument that deserves respect. Therefore, if you think like me of bruising as another road to spiritual growth, you find that it is very good to live according to this law.

Don't literally take it now. It's not threefold mathematically; it's more like an overall concept. A spell thrown out of wrath would probably generate even more wrath. So be very vigilant if you choose to execute some spells because there are repercussions. Trust me, and I was there—friendly advice: stay away from any form of black magic if you're a witchcraft beginner. Now, I'm not telling you ALL the magic of black is bad. To be frank, I think the dichotomy of black and white is a bit artificial. My point is, if you are a novice, you can wait until you have been more skilled in hexing and cursing because you can handle the downside from there. There are other ways to express your wishes. Be smarter than sorry.

Research a Lot

But don't confine yourself to reading. Look at Tumblr and Pinterest before buying a book. There are a lot of detailed books on beginning witchcraft, and it gives you a good sense of what a witch would take. Then the Amino App is an excellent place to learn more not only about printmaking, but also networking with other bruises worldwide.

Experiment a lot

I remember I asked you to do a lot of earlier research. The reality is, though, that witchcraft is not something you know from reading. It is a road. You cannot claim that you are a witch unless you do real kinds of rituals. Don't be scared to try new things. Only ensure that they are registered. Until you try a spell on the internet, always double-check whether it feels right for you. Your experience, as I said before, is your best guide.

Learn From More Experienced Witches

If you want to pursue witchcraft but don't know if you are ready, see if your area includes public rituals. Often they are coordinated into covens, witchcraft schools, or supernatural shops. Wait and watch. Wait. Note how it sounds; remember the execution of the high priestess or priestess.

You Don't Need to Own Every Witchcraft Tool

Apparently, witches can be very materialistic. But to continue witchcraft, you do not have all the equipment and all the exotic materials. The only resource you need to avoid witchcraft is yourself, and I have written a full post about this that you can find here. Yet I think you will find it simpler to execute spells and rites with certain basic tools as a beginner witch. Resources allow us to concentrate our thoughts and provide a tangible and sensory guide in our work.

Beware of premade witchcraft packs in the same way. Instead of buying a kit, you only have to get what you need for your spells and rituals. When I was going to cast my initial holy circle, for example, I'd just get a shadow book, an anthem, a cup, a red candle, and a little burning incense with a pack of frankincense sticks. And that's it. And that's it. Notice that you can find all this for a few bucks in a dollar store. It's a good way to start bruising without a lot of money.

Premade witchcraft kits can indeed be quite costly. In fact, you don't pick the items separately. So they won't work with your resources as well as if you had personally chosen them. Finally, you are going to purchase some other devices you like, so you are left with two of them, which can be very inefficient. Therefore, just buy what you need and nothing more for your charms. You will gradually build your altar and save a lot of space and energy.

Thoroughly Plan Your Spells and Rituals

Last but not least: prepare everything before you execute some spell (especially your first one). Use a map to select the best time to perform your spells. Use the moon, the sun, and the powers of the earth for your benefit. Choose paints, plants, stones, objects, and all components according to their meaning. Make it work for you (this is why I said you need a lot of research). Luckily, all good books on witchcraft are supplied by mailboxes, and many of them are available on the Internet, so you will find the information you need very quickly.

Practice Makes Perfect

I hope I haven't scared you off the witchcraft! I just think there are some things you should to before you launch. Here is another tip: if you want to become a powerful witch, practice is fine. Don't be afraid to try new things. Don't be frightened of making errors. As long as your intentions are pure, there can be nothing bad (it is a totally different game if you try black magic). If your conscience asks you to alter those spells, do it. If you feel obliged to do certain things, even if you can't find them in a book. Lookout and be imaginative! Imagine! The greatest witches rarely follow the letter orders. We act in accordance with their inner teachings and divine guides. You have to train and experiment to achieve this level of understanding and confidence.

Techniques for Training Your Mind

The imagination is the most important tool of Witchcraft— it works. Knowing how to practice your mind is a precondition for the art. The words, herbs, candles, tools, and movements are all there to help you focus and draw on your energy. They're not doing anything on their own.

What works out a spell is what happens in your mind. It is extremely important that you properly train your mind. The only real way to do this is by meditation.

Meditation Tips for When You Can't Sit Still

Meditation is a significant precondition for Witchcraft activity. Have you sought and learned to meditate on how good it is for personal growth and spirituality? Guess what? Guess what? You don't have to lie meditating either. Here are alternative ways to educate the mind.

Learn to Meditate for Beginners

Learn to meditate with a simple tutorial. Meditation is the basis for many religions, independent people, and healing rituals, such as Wicca. This book I discussed here brings meditation to the basics, helping newbies get going without getting overwhelmed.

How Meditation Helps Witchcraft

Meditation helps Witchcraft in many ways. This helps you to prepare your mind to achieve a goal over a long time, teaches you to consciously change your state of consciousness, enhances your pain capacity, and allows you to divide up feelings. Simply put, it is an elevated state of consciousness and will greatly benefit you when you practice the craft.

Grounding and Centering

Grounding and centering allow you to link your energies to the ground and concentrate on the planet. While everyone will benefit from studying these strategies, they are a must for beginners. In everyday life, these practices will help us.

Visualizations for Grounding and Centering

Visualizations for grounding and centering, and learning how to use them, can help make a living that is healthy, balanced, and not just in the ritual. These visualizations are a great way to achieve grounding and focusing in any case.

Advanced: How to Improve Psychic Abilities

Psychic abilities must be nurtured to learn and practice witchcraft. You must learn to develop your innate natural skills. I've provided some exercises to help you improve your psychic abilities.

Advanced: Energy Manipulation With Crystals

Energy modulation is an effective technique for any witch, but for beginners, it can be particularly difficult. In pagan religions or witchcraft, spiritual practices rely on your capacity to senses, collect, and project energy. Do you need to practice? Try these exercises to improve your skills.

Essential Skills for the Beginner Witch

To make your intentions work; learn the essential skills with which each beginner witch should be comfortable:

Cleansing, Consecrating, and Charging

Cleansing, consecrating, and charging are important for the art, also known as the "three Cs." If you ever read a Wicca book, you certainly have been told to do all these things— but you never really stopped thinking about what they are or what they are? Start to learn about the "three Cs."

Casting a Circle

Casting a circle is an art; just experience comes with it. These are certain techniques, tips, and exercises that you can use to develop your ability to carry out this essential Wiccan rite.

Great Magical Spells for Beginners

Spells don't just require executing a plot, as in games. You have to understand what you do. There are philosophies that you have to learn behind magic before you can trust it to work for you. If it was enough to readjust words of a page, then each actor playing a Witch on TV would shot fireballs.

Here are some basic forms of magic and spell casting "styles" that you can learn. The methods are reliable, and only a few items have to be modified for any reason. The more you train, the more professional you are.

A Beginner's Guide to Candle Magic

Candle magic is a magical kind of magic, perfect for beginners and powerful enough for advanced practitioners. Learn the fundamentals and start.

Petition Candle Magic for Beginners

The magic of petitions is a kind of candle magic that's perfect for new beginners. Learn how to create and use petition magic for any magical purpose.

How to Be a Kitchen Witch

For purposes of enchanting life, kitchen witches follow the craft and can have some religion or belief. We work with spices and household products to carry blessings.

Magical Potions, Brews, and Concoctions

Magical potions, brews, and concoctions all act as individualists. Learn the difference between each device type and the various uses it represents. Discover practical Witchcraft jargon, from mojo bag to witch bottle.

How to Cast a Jar Spell

Jar spells are highly versatile. The fundamentals can be learned here to use this technique for any magical purpose.

How to Cast a Witch's Ladder Spell

Witch's ladder spells are great for beginners, because no special instruments, recipes or intricate rituals are needed. They can be used at any time but are particularly suitable for use around the spring in a Beltane spell.

Pendulum Witchcraft

Pendulums are extremely useful instruments for Witchcraft practice and can disable other tools.

An Introduction to Blood Magic

The magic of blood always evokes every kind of gothic illustration. This is also a controversial subject in the supernatural culture. Figure out what you need to do and how to do it safely.

WITCHCRAFT MISTAKES BEGINNERS ALWAYS MAKE

Are you just beginning your Craft journey? When beginning any new practice, challenges and errors are supposed to be supernatural or mystical. Below, I have mentioned some of the most famous heartbreak mistakes.

Don't be too harsh on yourself if you have made one or more of these mistakes. I made some of them myself, certainly!

Being overly concerned with the details of a spell.

In order to achieve the desired results, newbies tend to look at a written spell and assume they have to replicate it correctly.

More like formulas than laboratory experiments, modern spells are. A button, a pinch. A pinch. But no two look alike as you share the photo on Instagram.

The detail-oriented spell casting is not accurate. Focusing on information creates energy and helps to make the purpose a reality.

Most witches like the color of their candles, the position of their compasses, incantations, and even the day and time of the week to conduct the rite. Nevertheless, it is more important to include things that have significance for you. Try to write your own spell, rather than attempting to replicate a spell exactly as it was written.

Not supporting spell work with mundane efforts.

Spell casting is about intent. So I guess it really makes a difference. I don't know how or why it works, to be frank. I believe it does. I think it does. But if you do not take that purpose into your real earthly life, it is unreasonable to expect "the World" to do everything you can.

So if you write a job, but never give a CV to prospective employers, your purpose is to do so. Yeah, half-ass pretty. Nonetheless, something can come along. Yet you naturally dramatically increase your chances by doing your part.

Spending too much money on ritual supplies.

As a homemade retailer of ritual materials, I see nothing wrong with witchy retail therapy every now and then. A fresh candle or statuary on the altar makes us happy. But the materialism of things shouldn't be your craft. You really don't need anything. Yet even if you want to work with resources, you actually already have everything you need.

Getting scammed.

This is not really a "mess" because it's not your fault if it happens. Nonetheless, I'm listed here, because it's important to know, especially if you start first and don't really know what to expect. The vast majority of heathen are decent, well-meaning people. But not everyone is above and beyond the use of the vulnerable, just like any other religious or spiritual group (including Christians, Buddhists, Hindus, Muslims, and others).

Run far and fast from anyone who:

- ✓ Makes unwanted sexual development in the social sense.
- ✓ Guarantee results from spells in exchange for money (especially love, money, and fertility spells).
- ✓ Claims that they have mystical "strength" or erratic skills.
- ✓ Offers to "break the spell" in exchange for money from your career.
- ✓ Pressures you to break family members' ties or make drastic changes to life.
- ✓ Claims to have "secret knowledge" only in exchange for money.

- ✓ Plays envy or animosity in seeking advice or information elsewhere.

There is no need to be more scared of these things than in a church or a synagogue.

While we definitely do not neglect innocent eccentrics, it is typically a very caring, supportive community.

Ethical heathens go to great lengths to avoid dishonesty because of the prejudices that mainstream society holds to them.

It is, in fact, the lack of awareness and education about modern witchcraft, which unfortunately draws criminals and scam artists who see the potential to profit from this ignorance.

Imposing one-size-fits-all beliefs on others because you read ... one book.

When your first non-fiction book about witchcraft has just been completed, bear in mind that you are at the beginning of a long journey.

There are several explanations of why and how magic works. Likewise, there are various hypotheses of legal witchcraft. Spare yourself some drama, don't give lectures about the' left-hand road,' or insist that the' three-fold rule' is a theory of some kind.

Be open-minded. Be open-minded. Please ask questions. Take everybody with a grain of salt— and try not to take yourself too seriously.

Assuming that all witches are Wiccan.

Ouch, it just makes me cringe to type it. The occult tradition encompasses an incredibly wide range of beliefs, from Louisiana's voodoo and Northern Europe's Celtic rituals. Only a small percentage of self-identified witches were Wiccans.

For the sake of God, please never use the words as if they are synonymous and look at certain other myths about witchcraft while you are there.

Being excessively anxious about coming out of the broom closet.

First of all, there's nothing you need to get out of the broom closet.

Most people of all faiths believe spirituality is a private affair. If you're that, I appreciate it.

And if you have a career or a public service, or live in a country that punishes witchcraft practices with serious legal sanctions, the miserable fact is that it doesn't always valuably "go viral." Yet 99 percent of the time, the societal ramifications of "coming out" as a witch are not almost as dire as you assume.

For many years now, I've been a very public pagan. I got conservative friends, liberal friends. I got liberal friends. I have profoundly Catholic, Jewish, and Muslim friends. We're traveling a lot and have mates on Earth from almost every populated world.

My child goes to a Catholic school, know what? What? Nobody's sending as &*! I'm a witch. I'm a witch. Others say it's strange or fascinating. I sometimes ask questions that make me chuckle. But nobody ever cut me off or shot me or kicked me out of a living room. This never happens, I'm not saying. It is probably not a good idea to tell a new landlord about your experience before signing a lease.

Discrimination is also an issue in the court system. The loss of work is a real risk to people in politics or monotheistic religious orders (family lawyers like pointing out that in custody cases, the mom is a witch). But this is much less popular than you probably think.

Ignoring social responsibilities or neglecting the Earth.

While witchcraft takes many forms, reverence for the earth is still almost universal.

Magic is a relationship of giving and taking with the world around you. When you take anything, you're expected to face some trouble. Express the demands by actively serving others and restoring the Earth.

Donate to charity, take volunteer opportunities, and feel the impact.

Not exploring the culture or tradition of a particular magical tradition.

If you want to use a spell that you know nothing, from religion or tradition, it has no context or significance.

Newbies seem to want to go right to the magic without taking the time to know more. If you don't even understand the incantation, an attempt to recreate an old Egyptian text spell is nothing but an awkward taste for a poor salon trick.

Do your work. Do your research. Spend time with those who know the culture and backwardness you are involved in. If possible, visit a temple or find a coven specialized in any type of magic you want to try.

FIRST STEPS TO BECOMING A WITCH: ADVICE FOR BEGINNER WITCHES

New Witch? Confused? Learn tips for witches for newcomers. I always say "comes home" as people come to witchcraft. That would make the simple art right off the bat. But it can be confounding, in fact. There's a lot of information about the art I didn't have when I grew up. There is sometimes so much detail that it is a daunting job to find out

First Step to Becoming a Witch: Read and Study!

First of all, it will almost always be the answer if you come to me and ask me where to begin witchcraft: What have you studied? When "nothing" is replied, then this is the first step. I saw many inexperienced witches asking for advice online, reading this or that book is told because they didn't like the advice. How do you expect to learn if you don't want to make efforts to research the subject?

Endless Resources for the Beginner Witch

Thousands of books on witches are out there. Here are a few places to find: Amazon online and other booksellers, thrift shops, book stores, and even the local library. If you cannot get books at your disposal, the best tool is–THE INTERNET. Google is the basic "early step to becoming a witch," and there are lots of websites on witchcraft. Search "How to make a rite of witchcraft" or "Pay a Ring," etc.

Write the basics down.

Note them down in a notebook or journal after you know the fundamentals. Learn them. Test them. When you learn enough about the fundamentals, and then continue to class. Keep in mind, even if you feel comfortable with the fundamentals, you never learn all about witchcraft. The idea is so large and so old (through thousands of years) that it takes many lives to know everything there.

Practice, Practice, Practice

The next moves towards becoming a witch require practice actually. When casting your first spell or conducting a rite, ask yourself the following questions:

- ✓ May I draw a circle and open it?
- ✓ Will I understand why I want to perform or cast this ritual?

- ✓ Do I understand the potential consequences of this practice if it comes to unwanted energy by chance from spell backfires or ritual?
- ✓ Do I know how to banish this unwanted energy?
- ✓ Was I evil because I am genuinely drawn to it, or just to spell somebody?

Your first spell...

My first suggestion is to write a spell in advance. Cunningham's World Magic Books have some fantastic spells and Judika Illes ' Anthology of 5000 spells. Keep the spelling simple: do not choose an ingredient or more spell than a few moves. You train, you don't show for an audience. Go on easily, and then when you master the fundamentals, you can pump up the volume. Once you have tried pre-written routines or spells, go ahead and write your own. You will find it will come to you as second nature.

Simple Magic to Practice for Beginner Witches

Sometimes you get the urge to spell, which needs little or no planning and minimal ingredients. For example, magic can be as easy as swallowing your negative energy with a broom from home! Weave the magic into your cooking: using spices, or draw patterns on your meal for specific reasons. As you grow and get acquainted with the unique energies of the craft, move the ladder of elaborate and difficult rituals. Try different things. Try different things. Don't be afraid to try new rituals and spells. And as with everything else in life, trial and error will happen.

Seek Connection With Nature

One of the key moves to become a sorcerer is to communicate with nature. It is important to have a connection to nature. Link to the Earth: plant a garden, walk barefoot, walk wildlife, pick up litters and help the rescues of animals. Link to Air: sense your hair's bride, reach the top of a mountain, breathe deeply, open the windows. Link to Fire: have a fire, light a candle every day. Water connects: go fishing, take a medicinal bath, and put small water well in your room.

The Importance of Nature Connection

Many witches online claiming that in their practice, they don't use the elements. All in and around us emerges from the elements. Do you practice the magic of candles? Smoke, Fire. Do you have an uncrossing bath? Water. I might go on and on. The idea is–you will see a difference in your spirituality when you interact with Mother Earth. You look like that mentally, too. Witches deal for nature every day because they know that everything comes from the Sun, everything goes back to the Earth. Your body, mind, and soul will continue to sync with the seasons, the moon, and the world in which you live. THIS makes you a mighty witch!

Focus on Energy

The essence of witchcraft is to control and exploit energies to change the environment and life of the witch. So one of the first moves to become a witch is to know everything about nature. All is life, and it never stops moving. Visualization and visualization help you to concentrate your emotional and mental energies on a goal. Practice energy manipulation–there are magical YouTube videos and online resources on this subject. Deal with crystals and just try to adapt to your particular strength, etc.

Connection With Ancestors

One of the first steps to being a wizard is to communicate with your ancestors. Now there are some new witches who are not going to agree that this is an aspect of the craft that they are not following. You have the option. But I'll tell you–even when I don't feel a bond with a god or goddess, I still feel the presence of my ancestors. In art, your ancestors are relevant because their blood pumps through you. Thousands and thousands have assembled to make you. Others claim it is pointless to look into one's origins or history, but I am here to assure you that your ancestors bring deep magic and security.

How to Connect with Ancestors

Using ancestry.com to link to your ancestors. Ask your family about your ancestors–their names, dates of their life, where they lived, etc. – and invite them to join your practice and secure your house. Simply create a shrine to your ancestors. Link your background, history, and myths (e.g., if you're primarily European, you could be a Celtic, Slavic, Roman, Greek, and Norse...)

Spirit Animals

Often when a beginner's witch comes to me, they want to know that their spirit animal is one step toward becoming a witch. You shouldn't think that's not a requirement. Your object in spirit must come to you. It's not the real spirit animal if you have to push it. When you're ready and in random places, the animal spirit will appear: in the wilderness, on tv, the internet, novels, conversations with strangers, etc. Your spiritual animal will come and go, according to the phase of your life.

Gods and Goddesses

Another big question from beginner witches is: how can I know my gods/pantheon? Start by looking at your ancestors. It's always great to learn and work with your ancestors ' gods. You will often receive gods and goddesses, just as your spirit animals will. When they do it, create an altar or a temple (no fantasy), worship the gods and make offerings, burn candles, burn incense, etc. as often as you can.

Diane J: Lockhart

A DEBUNKING OF COMMON MISCONCEPTIONS ABOUT WITCHCRAFT AS IT IS PRACTICED TODAY

It seems like everybody's witchcraft these days. More and more retailers are selling stuff like crystals and incense, witchy attire is portrayed by shows like American Horror Story, and astrological images are everywhere. Right now, the world is messy, so it's natural that people look for a little happiness in their lives.

As common as witchcraft, it's difficult to know where to begin. It can sometimes get frustrating with so many forums, books, and services. As someone who has practiced magic for many years, I get a lot of people asking how to get started, and I say that the "right" way to witchcraft is different for everyone. The magical thing about witchcraft is how rare it can be for different people. There are pitfalls and treats I saw when people first started witchcraft, and I mentioned them here to help all of the new witches continue their magical journey.

Note: Because witchcraft in many different cultures in the modern world takes many forms, I use the term "most" frequently, because there are certain deviations from each law.

I do not intend to speak of the diversity of witchcraft and paganism as a whole for any practitioner or pigeonhole, but rather to offer the meaningful counter position to common falsehoods about alternative spiritual ritual often labeled as' witchcraft.'

Witchcraft includes or is somehow related to devil worship

The concept of the "devil" as Western society is mainly derived from monotheistic Abrahamic religions such as Christianity and Islam. The belief in the devil as an enemy of the God of Abraham remains a holder of many faiths, and I absolutely respect that as a non-Christian.

Nevertheless, even western witchcraft practices do not consider a satanic entity.

The networks between mixed cultures in which Religious influence has characterized the concept of the devil, or those who classify themselves as "True devils," may consider an alternative entity known as "the devil." The devil is also acknowledged by most average Christians—that doesn't mean they worship him.)

Wicca and Witchcraft are the same things

Most non-practitioners interchangeably use the terms "Wicca" and "witchcraft." Since Wicca is relatively popular in the Western world, misunderstanding is easy to understand.

However, "witchcraft" is a broad word, and under it, Wicca and a variety of other beliefs, including Afro-Caribbean rituals, Celtic traditions, Central American traditions, and many indigenous practices around the world, are included.

Most Wiccans are not witchcraft to further the mystery. Spell casting is just one part of many, including moon cycles following, normal life, and the wheel of the year.

Typical Christians don't practice witchcraft

The priest is called to convert wine into the blood of Christ during a typical Mass, and bread into his body. This transition is expected to be symbolic for some. The transformation is even simply represented by many Christian beliefs.

In any case, many witches practice this and other traditional Christian rituals to spell craftsmanship or, at least, magic ritualism.

The aim of this analogy is not to offend Christians, but to find out that what witches do is not that different in shape at least.

We use ritual to connect with the sacred and spell craft as a means to show a higher power. Sometimes we even exchange the words "spell" and "prayer."

I mean no disrespect when you are Christian, and you prefer not to call your traditions "witchcraft." However, if you ask me what I call witchcraft, I really don't see much distinction between rosary and altar chants.

Also, "witchcraft" isn't a word for me. It's, therefore, easier not to be offended.

Witchcraft is an ancient religion

Witchcraft is an old practice. The earliest occupants of the cave left behind artifacts of shamanic light and described them as a universal archetype.

If we embrace the eloquent but simple definition of brightness in Wikipedia as' broadly.' The belief and faith in the supernatural abilities and skills of isolated people and communities "then practiced at once all the known cultures a sort of witchcraft.

Your forefathers have been witches. They've been witches to their ancestors. They just came down from witches. This is disputed by no professional archeologist or reputable human historian of any kind.

Even the Bible acknowledges the ancient roots of mankind in witchcraft.

Yet witchcraft is certainly not a religion. It is a feature of different religions, and many religions that freely accept their witchcraft use are, in fact, very secular (including, and perhaps particularly, Wicca).

If you let your kids spend time with pagan children, they may be converted or enticed into practicing witchcraft

Proselytism or' encouraged conversion,' however, with some major exceptions, is in a broad sense uniquely or at least most often employed by monotheism.

In reality, a monotheistic child is much more likely to try to convert a pagan child than elsewhere, for cultural as well as religious purposes. There's nothing wrong with that, I'm not told.

That's generally not how we roll, I'm just thinking.

Your kid might end up doing magic frightful stuff with his pagan pal, like stopping playing a half-hour video game to watch the stars or learning how to compost properly.

Yet casting a spell? Perhaps not.

Pagan parents usually experience sensitivity to non-paid parents as a community, and we recognize that you might not appreciate exposing your child to our beliefs.

Generally, we don't even suppose it's all right to perform a ritual with a pagan boy who is not ours. We have no universal doctrine; we can personalize our beliefs tremendously, even in the same partnership or community, from family to family. And we generally don't say what's all right for our families are all right for somebody else.

But if you have any misgivings, a simple, "We're glad to send little Jimmy off, but avoid theological subjects, because we tend to talk about these things with himself" will almost definitely fit well and make the argument successful.

Most notably, it is not acceptable to exclude babies, no matter how much you disagree with them, because of the religious or spiritual views of their parents. So don't. Don't.

Pagans/Witches are unattractive, ugly, socially awkward or otherwise make undesirable friends/partners

Damn. Many people may be stubborn.

Society has spent much for hundreds of years in producing strongly negative representations of pagans and witchcraft in general.

Think of the old, wart-speckled lady with gnarled and horrifyingly arthritic knuckles in her hats for a moment. (Is that something you should add to the feather? A few ribbons? A little color goes a long way, girl).

Today, the ultra-nerdy, overweight, pocket-marked middle-aged woman represents the new stereotype of a depressed, illusory human with a social life reduced and nothing else to do than decorate her home cats parade with exotic global crystals.

Like any other myth, these people exist to validate this idea of witchcraft if you look hard enough.

The most free, flamboyant, or articulate heathen acts as the most accessible, flamboyant, or expressive people in any society. We tend to cross the edges. We are generally very popular. And well, they still come off as strange.

You note these people because they're so visible and noisy, and you may feel like they're representative of the entire culture of witchcraft.

The professionals you consider most common, though, often have no privilege of disclosing themselves openly or even privately. We teach law, politics, or public school jobs that prohibit them from thinking about their activities publicly. And, they may think it's just a company for no one.

They're dressed as you do, they're going to Starbucks, and they're shocked! Apps they make ambitious plans for New Year and are worried about their dating life (also called "The Simple White Witch"). In short: in all other ways, they are mostly "natural." Or just as "natural" as any one of us gets.

Witches are resentful of, or generally intolerant around Christians

First of all, certain witchcraft practitioners consider themselves as Christians.

But if you had the unpleasant experience of being lectured by a pagan witch as a Christian, I am very sorry. This irony is humiliating to me.

I pray this isn't normal. This is not common. Remember that we're not all like that, at the very least.

If it helps, please note that many people use witchcraft after a bad childhood or early adult Christianity experience. This practice, not witchcraft itself, sheds light on their ideas and attitudes on Christianity.

No formal tradition, including Christianity, teaches hatred or intolerance of any religion. The best way to cure the bruises or misunderstandings of other people about your spiritual tradition is to be the best example you can humanly be.

A small drop of sympathy is easier to swallow than an ocean of anger or contempt. Let's all do a little harder to love each other.

Witchcraft is the only form of magic out there.

Many people have heard of witches, which renders them an available means of magic, not to mention the fact that the witch stereotype can give other women strength. After all, witchcraft is not for everybody, and there are plenty of magical ways and rituals. Determine witchcraft for your magical practice without checking any alternatives, like go to an ice cream shop and determine your first taste, without even asking for free samples!

You have to find a new god or goddess to worship.

Wicca has popularized the concept of a deity or goddess "patron" with whom you work in magic. Most people have them, and if you want to, go for them! Don't believe you've got to, though. Almost every faith has folk magic rituals, ranging from Christianity to Buddhism and Islam so that if you like, you can keep your religion and perform magic concurrently. If you don't want any part of God or religion, that's fine too! Some practices such as Chaos Magic say that you can do magic and do not work with "literal" gods.

If you call yourself a witch, then you are a witch.

This is difficult to understand for many people, but witchcraft is not just identification. It's nice you want to get going, and you've come so far on your way, but after a spell calling yourself, a witch is like calling a plumber after you've patched a leaky pipe. Thought for a while about the word witchcraft, it has a noun in it, which means it is what you're doing, not just what you thought. It's not up to me to tell you what precautions you will take before a certain magic procedure is called upon, what I know is that it's not so easy as changing your twitter handle.

CORE BELIEFS AND PRACTICES FOUND AMONG A VARIETY OF FORMS OF THE CRAFT

Beliefs of witchcraft are present in many cultures around the world, especially in Early Modern Europe, where witchcraft became a massive diabolical plot against Christians. Such prosecutions are better represented by European witch-hunts from the 14th to 18th centuries. Jean Bodin (1580) published a book in which he described fifteen attributes of a witch as part of the witch hunt. He put the following characteristics: God's rejection, denouncing God and other blasphemies, worshiping and sacrificing the devil, dedicating children to the devil, killing children before being baptized, giving Satan children yet in their womb, converting people into satanic cult, violating oaths swear in the name of the lord, polygamy, killing men and little children for creating broth; The term magic has long been associated with witchcraft in the English-speaking world due to this connection between the witch and magic.

Reo F. Fortune, for the first time, brought this difference to the light in his novel ' Sorcerers of Dobu' (1932) in which he described two distinct forms of supernatural human evil: magic, the dark magic of men, and the ancestral power of women. He proved that such convictions were useful in maintaining social order, but his explanations were validated by others no more than thirty years later, and his contribution to witchcraft and magic studies was finally accepted as groundbreaking and significant. Throughout his research of the Trobian islands, Bronislaw Malinowski (1954), the Ocean Anthropology guide, addressed similar findings, describing' corpse deviants and people attacking floating witches.' Similarly, the works of Evans-Pritchard (1937) have pioneered magic and witchcraft theory and have strongly separated them, showing in the cosmological assumptions the logic and rationality behind these views. Similarly, important research by Jane Belo (1949) from Bali, Beatrice Whiting (1950) between the Paiute and others, and Richard W. Lieban (1967) from Cebuano of the Philippines have also shown that there is pervasive anthropologic difference between magic and witchcraft and that elements of these traditions are strikingly similar all over the world. Shelley's Frankenstein; Stoker's Dracula; Irvens Sleepy Hollow; Shakespeare's "Macbeth," and even legends and novels from that postmodern period, including' Lord of the Ring,'" Harry Potter', and "Eragon' are only a few of the examples. Sir Walter Scott's' Ivanhoe;' Irving's' Sleepy Hollow;' Edgar Allen Poe's' House of Usher; Sir Walter Scott's' Ivanhoe.'

One who performs independently, without a family or a community, and without a common tradition. Sometimes they are part of the class of natural sorcerers who have developed their skills in previous lives.

There is a legend among witches that when a single soul performs "the maker" for several years, the experience is re-awakened when it becomes puberty.

Anthropologic Witchcraft

Anything that an anthropologist calls "witchcraft," usually referring to the following meanings:

1. The practices of individual (true or supposed) magic-users accused of at least sometimes using their magic outside the agreed cultural norms of their culture.

2. A perceived, sometimes unconscious status of being a demon that can threaten people with the "bad eye."

It is used by anthropologists and other researchers for spiritual belief structures, which operate outside the world's dominant traditions and have a belief in anomalies that are not taken into consideration by mainstream Western society. Such belief systems use natural and divine energy in healing and often approach life from an animistic point of view, believing that everything on Earth is alive, including inanimate objects.

Wicca – "A Religion"

Here at Black Witch Coven, it was important for us to talk about Wicca for several reasons:

- ✓ Some of our practitioners conduct Wicca today for reasons such as culture & covenant connections, ceremonial rituals and goddess worship, and pure pleasure.
- ✓ Many of us in Wicca had a base, and some of us have followed the mystical path.
- ✓ "Wicca" and the pioneers of the Wicca community have opened a big door for us all to the walkthrough! Wicca compelled the people to re-evaluate their views of witchcraft and magic (as sluggish as many seams), and now, in countries of the world, we can practice without fear of persecution.

So honor Wicca's teachings while you go back or into Wiccan rituals on your own long journey through spiritual life!

Wicca follows the ancient traditions of initiation and verbal instruction as a mystery religion, and its supporters believe it traces some of its roots back to and after Elusius ' mystery practices. As such, the practices of the British religious witchcraft can be seen as different from other aspects of the Wicca or Wiccan revival.

Traditional Wicca is best defined as: an Initiatory, a Magic-using, the Pagan Mystery priesthood, and a Horned God consort–celebrate its Mystery on the Eight Sabbats and the 13 Esbats.

Shaman (Natural) –

It can be questioned that shamanism is witchcraft or not. I'm here because shamanism is a kind of paganism. Shamanism stresses neither Christianity nor the pantheon. Shamans deal with nature completely: rocks, plants, birds, oceans, etc. Shamans well know Earth, their bodies and minds, and practice for many long years to fly and recover.

Warrior Witch

- ✓ Ruled by Aries and the Element of Fire
- ✓ Embodies the Archetype of the Warrior or Amazon
- ✓ Your magical gift is empowering self-love.

You have the heart of a warrior, and you are witchcraft expressing your ferocity. You are deeply linked to the element of fire and are determined to act and defend your loved ones and strangers alike. You have a strong sense of right and wrong (in your own belief system), and you're going to fight for that in which you believe. This can take the form of politics, political protest, or just defending people and ideas.

You have a natural affinity for defense and may feel very much called to serve with the goddesses of warrior-like Athena. One of your most critical tasks as a sorcerer is to find effective ways to channel your immense strength. You have the power to make big changes in the world, but sometimes you miss something to do with it. Fundamental technology should help you to understand more clearly the changes you want to see and to take more cohesive and deliberate steps in your life.

Many Warrior Witches have a powerful Aries signature, for example, Aries Sun, Aries Moon, Aries Rising, or Aries Dominant, but this is not a warrior witch!

Solar Witch

- ✓ Ruled by Leo and the Element of Fire
- ✓ Embodies the Archetype of the Sovereign or Queen
- ✓ Your magical gift is loving pride in yourself.

You're a witch who concentrates on the sun. The Moon is very attentive in the culture of witches, but you like to dine in the sunshine of a sunny day. Being outside is an important part of your routine, and you can enjoy outdoor activities throughout the day. The Sabbath is essential for your life, as it is based on the sun and, of course, on the summer solstice, the longest day of the year.

One of the greatest challenges you encountered as a sorcerer is interacting with the world, mostly involved mainly in the moon, midnight, and fall. Your tribe must also enjoy sunlight and heat!

Many solar witches in their astrological chart have a strong Leo signature like Leo Sun, Leo Moon, Leo Rising, or Leo Dominant, but this doesn't have to be a solar witch!

Wild Witch

- ✓ Ruled by Sagittarius and the Element of Fire
- ✓ Embodies the Archetype of the Healer or Wise Woman
- ✓ Your magical gift is acceptance and love for yourself.

You are a witch who is closely connected with nature's forest. This direction differs from garden witchcraft because you are interested in the forest, particularly, not only in the tamed order of a plant. You enjoy long walks in the forest and are the only people for kilometers. You are experienced in forging and enjoy making temporary altars in the park.

One of the greatest challenges you face as a sorcerer is to find this connection with the wilderness in your everyday life. It can be tough in our new 21st-century world to find the wild woman inside or even to find a green place to relax. Find ways to take your wildness to your house, wherever you go, will serve you well–communicate with the sound of a solitary bird singing in the woods on your way to work, meditate a few moments between meetings, and imagine wandering in a wild forest in the countryside.

Most crazy witches, such as Sagittarius Sun, Sagittarius Moon, Sagittarius Rising, or Sagittarius Dominant, have a clear signature in their astrology. Still, it does not have to be a mad witch!

Asian Traditions

The Shinto religion itself is a shamanist religion in Japan, and therefore the Japanese are not involved in witchcraft. In the Japanese language, the term "witch" is usually used as a person of high skills or prestige. Asian witchcraft traditionally focuses on the relationship between witch and animal or associated spirits, and in Japanese witchcraft, witches are usually divided into two categories: those with family snakes and those with foxes; the fox witch being the witch most often seen in Japan. Witches are often followed in China by scrolls, staff, and other devices similar to the Western rituals of witchcraft, in the shape of rabbits commonly identified with the Moon, fertility, and god. China's witches are famous for their extensive knowledge of the magical powers of plants and herbs, as well as their clarion and astrological research.

Pow-Wow Tradition

The concepts of "pauwau," which means dream seeker? Include shamanic practices, such as healing rites, dreams, and traditional medicine, frequently supplemented with prayers, incantations, songs, and dances. The term pauwau (pow-wow) was intended for the rituals and councils of the Native Americans because of their important role in both. The Pow Wow practice assigns great importance to the seeker as the bridge between group activities and rituals. While some claim the Pow-Wow culture originates in German, it is more a combination of Native American local traditions, and the practices of the German / Dutch pagan settlers settled in the United States ' Pennsylvania area.

Appalachian 'Granny' Tradition

A practice that dates back to the first settlers of the Appalachian Mountains who arrived from Scotland and Ireland in the 1700s in the USA and carried with them the spiritual practices of the "Old World." Those practices were then merged with the Cherokee tribes ' local tradition into a mixture of the local herbal medicines and charm, healing of faith, storytelling, and magic. The' granny' Witches are frequently called' doctor witches' or' wind witches' on whether they are more skilled in medicine and midwifery or if they are in more balance with nature, lay lines, and energy vortexes. This tradition is known as the' granny' since older women play a prominent role in mountain cultures.

Dianic Tradition

A blend of various traditions. The main focus is on the Goddess, who, in her three forms of Woman, Mother, and Crone, is worshiped. A "divine feminine practice," the covens are generally only for women. Dianic Witchcraft can be an outsider spectator, but it is an interwoven collection of practices that have influenced each other over the centuries and millennia.

Alexandrian

Alexandrian Witchcraft is a tradition that began in the late 1960s in Britain. With the reinvention of witchcraft by Gerald Gardner, Alex and Maxine Sanders created their own version. In Alex Sander's career, it shifted and transformed. Sanders characterized it as' slightly experimental,' focused on traditional ritual and ceremonial practice. Students were supposed to prepare as required and attend initiatory ceremonies.

Stuart Farrar, a Sanders pupil, wrote the popular book "what the witches do," which was still in print today, based on the Alexandrian Coven. Farrar refers to their form of witchcraft as Wicca, and I like this quote, especially: Wicca puts a great deal of focus on the reasons I have described. But Wicca's strength is its flexibility. Rigid dogma, conformism, and monolithic nature are foreign to their heart. Wicca's basic unit is not a single section, but the actual bond and the people who make it up. Every coven has its own style, character, focus, and commitment. The typical mine is so rich that every coven will create its rock. —Stuart Farrar: What do you witch?

British Traditional Witchcraft

British Witchcraft Traditional has too many variants to mention here. From the wise woman, old village sweetheart, to ritual magicians. British witchcraft is typically based on local beliefs and variants.

Traditions vary wildly from Ireland, England, Scotland, Wales and the Isle of Man. We also vary within those nations, territories, counties, and villages.

I was born in Cornwall, for example, where the wise men and women have a very strong tradition. We have been recognized as an intrinsic and essential part of society, known as pellers or pellars. Real, several frauds prevailed among them. And sometimes someone was falsely (or rightly) convicted so arrested for criminal witchcraft. Generally, people respected witches because they had accepted that insulting them was not a good idea; otherwise, bad luck would certainly follow.

Traditional British medicine was not mystical but relied on' the ancient' to assist with magical operations (and variations thereof). It's as relaxed as it gets. A typical witch may be practicing for a magical spell a long time, or she may simply speak a curse on the spot.

Chaos Magic/Witchcraft

A person who uses chaos magic (or magic) takes advantage of all other rituals. The word ' chaos magic' originated in the United Kingdom in the 1970s. The central idea behind it is trust: belief in the desired outcome and confidence in the way it is done. The main rule is that no rules exist. The ritual witchcraft could not be further mentioned above, yet it would use its components if the practitioner feels it could help.

A witch of chaos works on the same principle; taking different forces, techniques, and structures from different traditions heighten his belief in the assurance that it will be functioning and that he has complete faith in himself and the ability to change and construct his life.

The Hermetic Order of the Golden Dawn

This was an organization dedicated to supernatural research. In reality, the Golden Dawn was the first of three orders to rise in a hierarchy. The second was generally shortened to the Rosy Star, and the third the double leaders. Many of the Golden Dawn rituals and practices have been integrated into Wicca. It also shares other characteristics with Freemasonry since they were Freemasons, all three founding members. A very important distinction was that women were accepted from the outset as leaders.

Internal politics and conflicts devastated the Golden Dawn, and even if two off-shoot temples persisted until the 1970s, it more or less collapsed by the mid-20th century. Nevertheless, some types of order have been resurrected and are available online.

Satanic witchcraft

As a response to recent allegations of witches' cohorting the devil, satanic witchcraft arose. Its roots lie in America, but the phenomenon has spread worldwide with the advent of the internet. Satanism is a cult of mistrust against the structures of a dictatorial state. If you're for it, it's the typical satanic witch. We claim that no one without their permission can have jurisdiction over another.

Satanic witches live by seven tenets:

- ✓ Live with compassion.
- ✓ Justice for all is the ongoing goal.
- ✓ A person's body is inviolable.
- ✓ The freedoms of others must be respected.
- ✓ Beliefs should be in alignment with current scientific thinking.
- ✓ People make mistakes. We should right our wrongs.
- ✓ Wisdom, justice, and compassion must always prevail.

Each of the above values is a guide designed to inspire righteousness and honor. Fair enough. Fair enough. Any day of the week, I will give my vote to a satanic witch over a politician.

Stregheria

Stregheria is an Italian witchcraft type. It's got a lot together with Wicca. In recent years, the writer Raven Grimassi has brought Strega notoriety. Both professionals, however, do not agree with its style, and there seems to be a great deal of tension between different factions. I'm always in my ward when I see warnings on blogs to take care of the other sites that offer "misinformation." Acceptance of everything seems to me to be paramount.

The Italian-American Leo Martello first brought Stregheria to the notice of western pagans in the '70s. Since then, the texts and experience of Grimassi have moved the trend forward.

Druid

The modern or neo-Druid witch has great respect for nature and the druidic way of life. Druids also associate with Celtic society as representatives of conservation organizations. Many Druids say that their heritage was unbroken back in ancient times, but that has no evidence. Moreover, the ancient Druid rituals and experience have never been recorded, so modern Druidry is a reconstruction attempt. You've got a lot of fun.

Green Witch

A Green Witch interacts with and works with Mother Earth's powers. Through their ceremonies and practices, they also make use of natural objects and locations (such as sacred oak trees or lakes). You do this so that you can be closer to the Holy Spirit that you can perceive in nature. A Green Witch usually makes her realistic materials such as flowers and grasses and is much related and naturally rooted.

Nevertheless, some scholars differentiate witchcraft from witchcraft by finding out that witches often are assumed to have innate mystical powers, whereas sorcerers are considered average individuals with professional techniques. Different cultures have no consistent witchcraft model, frequently fusioning certain ideas such as magic, magic, philosophy, mythology, spirituality, science, and diabolism. (Britannica Encyclopedia, 2009) Many African and indigenous peoples around the world have the same dichotomy of magic and witchcraft.

Beliefs and practices related to witchcraft and magic have long been fundamental to human history. Throughout various parts of the world, many still believe in the dark powers of magic, such as the evil eye, while in many cultures, magic spells and rituals of treatment, safety, and good fortune is a routine matter. For part of the world, like Europe, the old faith for magic was replaced by ideas and views of modern science, which are fundamentally different from old conceptions only in the last few decades. The European witch-hunting period was a relatively short process in the history of witches and magic.

"The Art" is a much older way to describe the so-called Witchcraft. But some say that "Art" is, in essence, the art of magic or technology that is not unique to or used by pagan religions.

Witchcraft was guilty of both men and women. Also, Malleus Maleficarum, the infamous witch-hunting book, used pronouns from both sexes to describe and identify witches. The Malleus also included statements such as "Nothing hurts the Catholic faith more than midwives." However, figures suggest that the overwhelming majority of executed victims were women (82%) during the time of most persecution (1500-1700).

An estimated 75 to 85% of those accused in early modern witch trials were female, and misogynies on the part of the witches who were persecutors are certainly demonstrably demonstrated, obvious from quotations like'[It is] not unreasonable that this specter of humanity,[witches] should mainly be drawn from feminine sex' (Nicholas Rémy, c. 1595) or' The Devil uses them as he knows this

Nevertheless, the so-called misogynistic nature of the witchcraft plays was fought over by the systematic reproduction of a few of the relevant parts of the Malleus Maleficarum. Many modern scientists argue that witch-hunting can be interpreted as an example of male misogyny in a simplistic way, since other women have been often accused by women to the point that witch hunting, at least at a local level, has been described as motivated primarily by "female quarrels."

Barstow (1994) argued that, given the same charges against women and men, a mixture of variables that included greater value placed on men as workers in the increasingly wage-oriented economy and greater fear of women as inherently evil filled women's scales. Thurston (2001) saw this as a part of the general sexism of late medieval and early modern times that had developed from the early medieval period during what he described as the "persecuting age." Gunnar Heinsohn and Otto Steiger hypothesized in a 1982 book that Witch hunts target women trained in the kinship field in an attempt to extinct awareness of birth control and to "repopulate Europe" after the Black Death demographic tragedy.

CLEAR DISTINCTIONS BETWEEN WICCAN, TRADITIONAL, AND ECLECTIC PATHS

WICCA

Wicca is a new, occult-based movement, practiced mostly in the West. It is based around the middle Ages on pagan practices and beliefs prevalent in Western and Northern Europe before Christianity took root. Current Wicca practitioners are predominantly women and girls because the faith centers on women's strength and goddess worship. Wicca is rooted in the old English term wicce, which means "to transform or mold something for the good of you." Wicca's witchcraft is based on this concept.

Wiccan Beliefs and Practices

Wicca is usually theistic, honoring two gods: the goddess and the creator. God is the primary deity in more conventional Wicca communities. But in more modern and feminist groups in Wicca, the Goddess is the principal goddess or sometimes the only deity known.

Traditionally, Goddess is identified with moon, star, and sea powers, while God is affiliated with the sun and forests. The goddess is also seen as the mother god.

Wicca followers concentrate their adoration on one or both deities as well as natural elements. Witchcraft, incantations, and divination rituals (usually by tarot cards) are important aspects of Wicca as well.

It is difficult to identify particular comprehensive Wiccan values because there is no single definitive text that all Wiccans abide by. There are also many different groups reflecting the Wiccan faith. Wicca relies more on practice than adhering to any particular doctrine or truth (witchcraft, rites, ceremonies, etc.). Nevertheless, most Wicca practitioners have some basic beliefs and practices.

- Wiccans practice eight regular Sabbaths with rites and rituals.
- The Elements: Earth, Wind, Fire, and Water, together with the fifth element of Spirit found in the other elements, are revere. Environmentalism is, therefore, often an integral part of Wicca.
- Wiccans consider magic not only as a belief in the supernatural but as the deliberate manipulation of natural elements.
- "Harm zero" is the most widely held rule in Wicca.
- The three-fold law of Wicca is another common rule that refers to karma. The Threefold Law states that whatever spells a witch sends out will come back three times.

- In part, because of its freedom to embrace and borrow from other faiths, the Wicca faith does not actively promote the evangelization of others.
- Reincarnation or regeneration following a death is practiced in the Wiccan faith.

Wiccan Symbols

- Pentagram: This is a Greek word meaning "five-pointed star." Although the pentagram has been a metaphor for several millennial sects, in Wicca, each of the five objects reflects the five elements: the earth, sun, fire, water, and spirit.
- Pentacle: this word is both Greek and Latin. This word has its origins. A pentacle is a pentagram with a circle around it, and a pentagram has a similar meaning. The circle represents white magic for some Wiccans, which is considered to be harmless.
- Sigil: It's a word in Latin that means' a sign, a mark, or a seal.' These are not set, official symbols, but generated symbols that can be used by magic. Sigils are designed in various ways (using letters, numbers, and/or images), but when the symbol is on paper, Wiccan concentrates his intense feeling on it by staring at it and then destroys it to release its power.

Wiccan Spells

Natural forces are believed to be used in rituals of Wicca to achieve the desired result. A spell is usually made with a mixture of spell-specific incantations, acts, and ingredients.

Wiccan magazines encourage pre-written spells, but Wiccans can also write their own so as not to break the Wiccan expression and remember the rule of the three.

Witchcraft Traditions

There are several different systems and practices of spiritual beliefs in the pagan community that fall into the varying headings of Wiccan, Neo Wiccan, or Pagan. But many simply identify as witchcraft rituals in the Wiccan sense. Here are some of the most frequently discussed communities you will find when you encounter people from different Wiccan or Neo-Wiccan cultures. There are different types and patterns of practice of witchcraft— some may not be appropriate for you and others. Read about theological changes among Wiccans and Neo-Wiccans— some of these differences can surprise you!

In an attempt to overcome uncertainty, Gardnerians and Alexandrians in North America (this includes anyone that can trace their initiatory lineage back to Gardner or Sanders) started to call themselves "English mainstream Wicca." This seems to be partly because there are so many other traditions called Wiccans that can not necessarily trace their lineage to Gardner or Sanders. Across Europe, where there are fewer alternative Wicca traditions, the word "English Traditional Wicca" was not commonly used. Throughout Britain, the word "initiator Wicca" is generally referred to by people like Gardnerian and Alexandrian Wicca, but even this term is misleading because in England, there are other witches with history and campaigns that identify as Wiccan. The vocabulary thus remains complex and ambiguous.

Eclectic paths

Eclectic Wicca is an all-inclusive term for the traditions of witchcraft, often Neo Wicca that does not fit any particular definitive category. Most Wiccans follow an eclectic direction, but also covens are considered eclectic. For a variety of reasons, a coven or a person may use the word "eclectic." For example:

1. Mixed and matched customs: a group or individual may use a combination of convictions and practices from various pantheons and traditions.
2. Modified traditions: a community could have been the offshoots of a well-established Wicca tradition, such as Gardner or Alexandrian, but would have to change the custom substantially from that of the original.
3. Different traditions: An individual may create his or her own values and practices tradition, and as this culture cannot be identified as something else, it is usually described as eclectic.

4. Uninitiated practitioner: A solitary person can use oath-bound, initiatory knowledge but does not use what he or she has learned from publicly available literature on Wicca.

Eclectic paganism is the epitome "no dogma," which is the tradition of paganism most often practiced by solitary pagans or pagan people who are not part of a tree or grove that are two kinds of pagan congregations. It is a pagan path that derives from a range of traditions. Odin and Athena can be worshiped, through Celtic rites. They may also observe a unified pantheon or follow the guidelines of another pagan tradition, but develop their rituals and practices. Eclectic paganism, even by pagan insiders, is difficult to define, since there is no formal orthodoxy of paganism. As such, the distinctions between cultures are blurry, and it is difficult to decide who draws from several traditions.

It is difficult to define pagan religions because there is no fixed doctrine that says, "this is what being a druid means." Rather, hepathians are allowed to find out for themselves what it means to be Wiccan or Eclectic. Defining Pagan traditions is often an individual matter and a sensation to the annoyance of interested outsiders. A Wiccan may not have a perfect definition of Wicca, but he does know his faith sufficiently well to look at something and say "this is not Wiccan" or to feel the energy of the ritual of a different person and know that he looks at a Wiccan sister.

Since there are sometimes disputes over who is Wiccan and who is not, confusion between current Wiccan boundaries and recent diverse practices can arise. Some people would say that Wiccan can only be called lineage covens (based on traditional practices). By this reasoning, anyone who claims to be eclectic, by definition, is not Wiccan but Neo Wiccan. Note that the term Neo Wiccan simply means someone who practices a newer Wicca and is not intended to be derogative or insulting.

Differences

There is a big difference between traditional folk witchcraft and Wiccan tradition Folk witchcraft does not classify as Wiccan and appears to investigate the mysteries of Lucifer and Christianity alongside Pagan mysteries. The Wiccans tend to concentrate on the Lord of Horn and the Moon and don't use the word "Devil." A high priestess and high priest are leading Wiccan covens. Folkloric covens normally have a tutor and a cook. In this book, I have therefore suggested whether a tradition is witchcraft or Wicca.

There are so many witchcraft traditions that they are hard to list. I have listed the customs in alphabetical order in this appendix in order not to suggest hierarchy. Some of the customs are mentioned in this section as they have similar names, which can cause confusion. There is a list of practices with more information on different traditions of witchcraft.

Wicca and traditions

1734 witchcraft

Joe Wilson founded the custom of 1734 following a long correspondence with Robert Cochrane, founder of the Tubal Cain clan. It is a heritage of folk craftsmanship. She also uses riddles to spread her mysteries.

Alexandrian Wicca

Alexandrian Wicca was founded in the 1960s by Alex Sanders. Sanders was introduced to Gardnerian Wicca, although he has a second degree or not. The definition of ceremonial magic appears to include more than Gardnerian Art. Gardnerian and Alexandrian initiates in the UK and Europe can visit the circles of each other, without having to re-initiate.

Clan of Tubal Cain

History of tribal witchcraft. The clan is the lines-bearers of Evan John Jones' Robert Cochrane family. The clan is also regarded as God's man. We are a closed group of Initiatives associated with the Shadow mysteries inside the Luciferian Sea of knowledge. The Clan of Tubal Cain's religious values are Reality, Love, and Beauty.

Dianic Wicca

A radical and gender-centered Wicca, founded in 1971 by Z Budapest. Women are not included in the form of witchcraft, and transgender women are usually excluded from their circles. Dianic Wiccans are monotheistic goddesses who worship the goddess as the center of all creation.

Feri Tradition

A type of traditional American witchcraft originating from Victor and Cora Anderson's teachings and transmitted by their separate initiates. Feri aims to turn the human through ceremonial healing, meditation, and energy practices. Huna, Conjure, Voodoo, Tantra, Celtic magic, Christian mysticism, Yezidi myths, and Greek gnosis are sources of Tradition. The Feri philosophy has recently separated itself into two strands: firstly, it is claimed that mysteries can only be learned in small experiential and initiatory groups, and secondly, that healing can be practiced in large groups by schools. The main argument in the break was the matter of charging money for training.

Gardnerian Wicca

Gardnerian Wicca was founded in the early 1950s by Gerald Gardner and traced its roots back to the covenant of New Forest, including Dafo,

Mother Sabine, and the family of Mason. Doreen Valiente wrote much of his early liturgy. In Gardnerian Wicca, there are several lines with a significant difference in spirituality between them. Gardnerian Wicca's focus is less formal than Alexandrian Wicca.

Georgian Wicca

George (Pat) Patterson, Zanoni Silverknife, and Tanith formed the Georgian Tradition in 1970. It started as a little coven in Pat's Bakersfield, CA. Pat was taught early by Scottish members in Boston. In 1970 Pat began a magic call, which led Zanoni and Tanith to find him and to help establish the Georgian tradition. The covens in British Columbia, California, Florida, Oregon, Colorado, Pennsylvania, Ohio, Washington, and Oklahoma are well-known.

The inclusive Wicca tendency

The Wicca inclusiveness, but rather trend in current practices. Any Wiccan should identify as multicultural and work towards through their practice towards LGBTQIA+, disabled and Black people, indigenous peoples, and vibrant people. A holistic philosophy towards Wicca encompasses eco-spirituality, psychology, attitudes towards reality, the sacred, morality, a culture of consent, group dynamics, covenant government, ceremonies, ethics and theology, and Wiccan practice, history and magic, and how they can be explored as part of a liberal religious approach to Wicca.

Inclusive Wicca Tradition (Australia)

After several years of learning the Craft from a variety of sources, Amethyst Treleven created Inclusive Wicca. After three different traditions and having completed a PhD degree in Wicca, which allowed her to participate in a wide variety of pagan practitioners, she saw both Wicca's good and not the good. To herself, she wanted more, and to her fellow Wiccans, she needed more.

McFarland Dianic Wicca

A Dianic Wicca offshoot that is usually open to bisexual women and men. McFarland Dianic is a neopagan worship ritual founded by Morgan McFarland and Mark Roberts, who have a separate faith and allow male participants in some instances despite their shared name. The McFarland legacy is based largely on Robert Graves ' novel The White Goddess. Although some McFarland covens accept members, their leadership is limited to female priestesses. McFarland Dianic covens, like other Dianic traditions, are female.

Minoan Brotherhood

The Minoan Brotherhood was founded as a backlash to the heterosexist ideology of most types of mainstream bruising in the 1970s. In 1975 in New York City, Edmund M. Buczynski founded the Brotherhood. Eddie was a Gardner and New York Welsh elder and a Wicca family building elder. The Minoan Brotherhood is a masculine initiatory practice of a craft that celebrates life, love of men, and magic. It is mainly based on the Cretan, Egean, and ancient myths of the Near East.

Reclaiming

Reclaiming is a community of people who strive to unify politics and soul. Their dream is grounded in the theology and spirituality of the Immanent Spirit of Life Goddess. They see their work as teaching and magic: the practice of inspiring one another and ourselves. They train their voices, bodies, energy, intuition, and mind in their classes, workshops, and public rituals. Students use the skills students learn, both as people and as a group, to express their concerns about the world in which we live and to give birth to a new culture dream. The Reclaiming movement, established around the year 1980 in the San Francisco Bay area, now encompasses hundreds of national groups in North America and Europe and Australia. The founder of Reclaiming, Starhawk, was taught by Victor and Cora Anderson in the Feri tradition.

Diane J: Lockhart

ECLECTIC WITCHCRAFT

The definition of an eclectic witch is one of the most difficult magical traditions to describe, except for the fact that the word eclectic means different things. Quite simply put an eccentric witch is one who practices more than one tradition and uses various paths, cultures, and traditions in her work.

Confusion arises as we speak about how various supernatural mechanisms can be combined to have a positive effect. There are some differences between a sorcerer who is familiar with two or three different traditions and who blends the parts of each one of them into a unified whole which is her way, and a witch who takes the strange idea here and there and throws them all in haphazardly the random pot, without trying to grasp the culture and history behind each traditions. Without understanding why a magical practice is pertinent to a tradition, absorbing this practice in individual work is useless, and a witch who chooses to do so won't benefit much. However, it is important to understand that certain paths are very compatible, and an eclectic witch who uses paths from a similar field may find it helps her to develop her own path.

To some degree, many modern witches show a degree of eclecticism, and one can argue that the witch does not miss, as it is hard to imagine any tradition that could not be enriched by other people's ideas and practices. The difficulty of being eclectic comes when unharmonious systems are combined, and an insufficient understanding of ideas from all different systems is not sufficiently understood. It would not risk the work of such a witch, but it would make it quite useless. One of the most important things to learn about magic is that it works once you understand why. Random ingredients use, because they have meaning for a witch on another road, but mean nothing to you. There is also the risk of being over the diversified-the root of every culture with which it works dilutes a witch who wants to study, learn, and work with everything. With no continuity between the mysterious paths, it will inevitably become a pick-and-mix of irrelevant fragments in its own direction.

The idea of being diverse can be generalized to match the notion of a tradition that changes over time. Even the most traditional family traditions change and develop with the birth and addition of new family members. There is (at least as far as I know) no single word that describes a witch who practices a primary tradition that encourages her to evolve and change. In the absence of such a word, we call them eclectic. Strictly speaking, they don't suit the term, but they reiterate the notion that witchcraft can't hold still and that fresh thoughts and feedback are required to prevent either direction stagnating.

Eclectic Wicca is a different concept than Eclectic Witchcraft, although the idea of choosing various elements from various sources also holds.

A hybrid Wiccan may combine Alexandrian and Gardnerian or even merge one Wiccan style with another mystical path. Where Eclectic Wicca cannot be used as a term is when an individual's practice does not confirm the structure established by the Wiccan religion. You can't claim to be Wiccan, for starters, if you don't believe in god. Unlike witchcraft, Wicca is a given mystical experience with certain beliefs. A person who does not hold the fundamental beliefs cannot claim to be part of the religion.

Reasons for Using the Term Eclectic

The word is used by solitary or covens in the event that:

- ✓ A community is an offshoot of a tradition of Wicca, such as the Alexandrian or Gardnerian, but has adapted their approach by no longer in accordance with the tradition of the majority.
- ✓ A single person or group can use a mixture of practices and beliefs from different traditions and pantheons.
- ✓ A solitary person can practice what he or she has learned from a publicly available source on Wicca without using eclectic oath-binding induction materials.
- ✓ A solitary person can establish their patterns of thought, practice, and because no current standard can define or add the culture, it is certainly considered eclectic.
- ✓ The controversial membership of the Wiccan community.

Because of the question of who is a genuine Wiccan or not, a problem with new diverse practices and Wiccan beliefs emerges. Many people encourage only lineage Covens to be called Wiccans, while the others, who tend to be diverse, should be considered Neoviccans and not Wiccans. Neo Wiccan is a term that refers to Wiccans who practice new practices which are not recognized traditionally.

Lineage For The Eclectic

Lineage is a term used to describe the person who initiated a Coven and initiated the person who initiated a Coven; it is a kind of Lineage. There are practices where lines are very significant, and the absence of a legacy makes a coven a Neo-Viccan and not an actual Wiccan. To stop that, you should take your lineage seriously and write it down. While it is not important for some cultures, it is very important for those who consider it. When a legacy is disputed, individuals are unable to claim magical ancestry that they do not have the right to claim. The members of a family have no duty to show their ancestry to people who are not part of the tradition.

The Neowiccans are considered diverse because the beliefs of their practices are not completely practiced. In most cases, they deviate from their beliefs and seek to mix them up with some modernization.

Can Eclectic Witches practice in a coven?

Of course!! Of course! Many eclectic witches successfully practice covens, which share the same open mind and adaptability, instead of a prefabricated structure. Although traditional covens have up to 13 members in general, an Eclectic coven could have as few or as many members as it feels right.

CORE CONCEPTS UNDERLYING THE "WHY" AND "HOW" OF MAGIC

WHY

- ✓ Magic is a precision science! It is also:
- ✓ The science of deliberate creation.
- ✓ The science of effective prayer.
- ✓ The science of manifesting Higher Will (God's Will) on the energetic and material planes.
- ✓ The science of heightened awareness, selective perception, and dynamic, harmonious relationships.
- ✓ The study of intention (as per Aleister Crowley, one of the greatest magicians).
- ✓ The system of creation, not coercion.

Note: The term manipulation is often used together with magic, but manipulation means simply the use of the hands. It should be an "OK" term, but at present, it is mostly used to indicate coercion. Look up! Look up! Look up!

Each deliberate act is a magic act! Magic allows us the capacity to interact with people on all levels and helps us to understand the actual workings of the world through direct experience.

Magic is the traditional path of spiritual growth.

Magic isn't unusual knowledge. It's the "normal" way of living. We have lost access to it just now. If you grasp this form of knowledge, you will answer theological problems that otherwise are catechism. The catechism is not appropriate from the point of view of a magician since a magician must observe and test everything for himself. It avoids the dogma trap. In the past, it was important to have a mystical base so that we could go and talk to Jesus, the Devil, etc.

Magic is necessary for effective religious practice,

A priest is eligible in religious practice to perform rites but not to establish them. Only the magician can create because he has the tool to check the routines he makes. There is some uncertainty about how to spell the term "magic": magic, magic, and technology. There are three widely known features. The first method used by Eliphas Levi is "magic" to differentiate between religious or ritual magic and stage magic.

Nature And Scope

Magical practices include divination, astrology, incantation, alchemy, witchcraft, spirit therapy, and necromancy. The term magic in Western popular culture is also used colloquially to refer to works of conjuring and entertainment. The purpose of magic is the acquisition of wisdom, power, love, or richness; healing or avoiding sickness or danger, ensuring that an adversary can be created or succeeded; revealing information; causing spiritual transformation; tricking and entertaining. The magic's efficacy is often determined by a magician's state and performance, who was supposed to have access to unknown powers and special knowledge of the words and actions necessary to control them.

Magical related practices include mysticism, healing, paganism, atheism, witchcraft, shamanism, voodoo, and superstition. Magic is sometimes split into the' strong' magic that verges on science and the' low' magic of ordinary folk traditions. There is also a distinction between "black" magic, used for unjust reasons, and "white" magic, generally used for good purposes. Although these boundaries are often ambiguous, it's because of the spiritual power that is expected to be channeled through the practitioner who, in some cultures, is a marginalized or stigmatized individual and in others a central figure that has a sense of "otherness."

Ten Benefits of Learning Magic

The art of magic is not just for entertainment but inspires people to be sufficiently creative in their own lives. Even if you aren't a magician, you can still make a difference, taking advantage of the magic art.

1. It helps develop self-confidence and increase confidence.
2. Curiosity, creativity, and imagination are encouraged.
3. It enhances interpersonal skills such as the ability to present, connect, and speak publicly.
4. This refers to the growth and synchronization of fine and gross motor skills.
5. Enhances critical thinking and problem-solving skills.
6. Constructs self-discipline.
7. You become the attraction point in group meetings.
8. Change the way you look at things.
9. You will amuse, entertain people, and happily delight them with magic.
10. Magic can be a good income source.

Functions

The "instrumental" and "expressive" functions of magic play are primarily among the many positions. Depending on its attempt to influence nature or human behavior, the instrumental role of magic is calculated by its success in achieving the desired outcome. Three major forms of magic are known by anthropologists: positive, defensive, and harmful. Productive magic is used to achieve successful results, such as good hunting or harvest or good weather, from human labor or nature. Protective magic seeks to protect an individual or society from nature's vagaries and other evils. The use of amulets to deter infectious diseases or to chant charms before a ride were evidence of this preventive feature. Finally, destructive magic or witchcraft is meant to harm others, is often motivated by envy, and is socially disruptive. The use of counter magic toward magic could thus reduce social tension in a culture.

The expressive purpose of Magic comes from its symbolic and social significance, although its practitioners may not be conscious of this position. Magic can give members a sense of group identity through shared rituals that give power or strength. At the same time, the magician can be alone within or at the margins of society as a special person. Magic can also be used as an innovative multimedia source. It is thus inseparable from the whole structure of thought, perception, and action in a given society.

Elements of magic

Spells

Magic includes words and abstract numbers that are meant to have innate power, divine or human material artifacts, and ceremonial acts carried out by the sorcerer or other people, such as spells, incantations, or charms. A spell or incantation is supposed to draw the power to perform spells from divine institutions. Knowledge of kinds or abstract numbers is often hidden and can be admired or hated by the owner of such knowledge.

In some cases, the potion is the most important component of the sacred ritual or ceremony. For, e.g., the Trobriand Islanders of Melanesia found that using the correct words is important to the success of the ceremony. Among the Maori of New Zealand, words are considered so significant that errors are assumed to cause a tragedy for individuals or the society in public recitations. In comparison, like the European medieval magic that used ancient languages and parts of the Latin liturgy, spells also use obscure jargon that relates to the rites revered. In many faiths, belief in the healing power of words is also widespread. Shamans, celestial mediums and mystics, for instance, echo specific sounds or syllables to attain an exalted state or an elevated state of consciousness with their spiritual strength. And new magic in entertainment with its use of the word abracadabra retains the latent charm.

Material

Most anthropological literature refers to the magical items used as "medicines," thus the common use by magicians of the term medicine man. These medicines include plants, animal parts, gemstones, sacred objects, or entertainment tools, which are deemed to be effective in them or activated by incantations or rituals. In some cases, the drugs intended for cure are physiologically effective; for example, cotton is commonly used as an anesthetic, Chinese willow bark as an antibiotic, and Medieval Europe used garlic and onions. Many drugs, including toad extracts and bufadienolides, are known to be toxic. Many materials have a symbolic connection to the desired result, as with animal parts divination. In Scapulamancy (sheep shoulder bone divination), for example, the sheep bone reflects the universe's macrocosmic forces. In magic, a witch is allowed to use something that belongs to the intended victim as part of a ritual (i.e., nails, nail parings, or clothing). The ritual itself may be symbolic, like making defensive circles where ghosts are to call up, sprinkling water on the earth to rain, or smashing a wax photo to harm a person. Plants or other items can also symbolize desired outcomes: the Trobriand uses the light vegetable leaves to make it easier for the vessel to float across the river in rites to guarantee canoe speed; the Zande of South Sudan put a pillar in a tree barrel to delay sunset, and several Balkans swallowed gold to cure jaundice.

HOW

The Four Elements of Air, Fire, Water, and Earth

There are many ways to develop magical and shamanic abilities. Nevertheless, at the base of all these routes, the four elements of magic are known: air, fire, water, and earth. One of the fundamental principles of magical studies is that all in this world consists of a mixture of these four elements, and if you understand and know how to work with them, you will understand (and create) anything you want.

Therefore, the magic of four elements is the first field for our apprentices–it is at the center of the entire world, including magic powers and abilities. For starters, you can learn clear-sightedness and telepathy by cultivating and using the water dimension, which means that the five senses have no access to knowledge. Water, being Spirit's tongue, lets you access almost any knowledge (or emotions) on a spiritual level. The levitation is the result of your air factor being raised, and your ground element reduced. And telekinesis is the ability to direct your fire energy to a certain object. We teach our students to use their telekinetic ability, for example, by tossing firebolts into a burning candle. You know you have begun to develop this skill by breaking and jumping the blaze by pointing your finger at it.

Nevertheless, beyond these spiritual or mystical powers, the four elements allow us to create and monitor our dreams of creation, to listen to the instructions of our Spirits, and to lead more imaginative and peaceful lives in general. By understanding the basic "building up" and rules that guide our world, we will learn to float instead of swimming upstream. This is the real value of four mystical ingredients.

Is it fun to develop magical abilities? Definitely! Absolutely! For self-defense, personal power, and much more, it is also useful. But it is also the culmination of a deep understanding of life's driving forces. This is an important first step on the path to direct knowledge and divine study.

When the shamans were thrown out of the tribe centuries ago, this direct knowledge was lost to the world. Now we need the shamans more than ever, and by learning the four elements of magic, we invite you to follow this path.

Magical Element Air

One of the fundamental principles taught by every apprentice magician or shaman is that almost everything in this world is comprised of a mixture of the four supernatural elements: air, fire, water, and earth. The premise is that if you can clearly understand the four elements, you can comprehend anything in the world.

The pupil also discovers that everything real and tangible has started in someone's mind as a mere thought, or, in this case, as the element Air. Air's at the start of all life, so you must start with Air if you want to create something. Air is linked to the East and elementary beings, also known as sylphs.

Air governs: seeing, breathing, speaking, listening, preparing, dreaming, believing, memorizing, talking, studying, teaching, knowledge, ideas, wisdom, and understanding.

What do you mean? What does that mean? This means you need to deal with the air factor if you want to influence any of these places in your life. Air is the perfect place to start practicing for an early magician. Air is strong as an item, but not harmful. Air is associated with three colors:

- ✓ Clear: respiration, physical reactions, bodily thoughts, vision.
- ✓ White: thought, thought, planning, communication.
- ✓ Sky Blue: divine light, insight, awareness.

And how can you use Air to control and enhance your everyday life? This is an easy way to start. We know from experience and observation that the color white activates the mental processes. You will not be able to think, know, or understand well if you have either too little or too much white in your elemental balance. If you are having difficulties in any one of those fields (or want a reference and can't seem to study), search your setting and your wardrobe for how much White is in it. When you see a lot of white people, change their clothes or change their place. Switch to a Sky Blue area or even Sun Yellow area. When the little White covers you, put on white clothes, or step into a room with white walls. In any situation, you will notice a change in mental pace and comprehension!

More About Sylphs

While in this world, it is true that almost everything consists of the four elements, the exception being elemental entities such as sylphs.

Elementary creatures are composed entirely of one element so that sylphs consist entirely of air. Sylphs are polite creatures with a body of around 3 to 18 centimeters in length. You enjoy playing smoke cigars or dust devils. Sometimes you may feel a sylphus like a light brush on your face. They're fun to be around and even make great messengers and information sources. We used sylphs during the fires to help us find safe routes through the park when we were driving through Yellowstone.

To connect with sylphs, pray for one in your head quietly. Sylphs have short lengths of attention, so it is better to communicate with your mind because the word you speak is too slow. Tell what you need and then give it on its way (thanks, of course, always in advance). Don't be disappointed if the sylph returns with the answer you need in short order!

Magical Element Fire

Fire is an action-based aspect of the process of development, which is also related to will, personal power, and imagination. Once you've developed the idea of what you want to build in the Air Element (and have done the planning part), it's time to move into Fire to take action and make a difference.

Fire is connected to the south, which is also the reason we are doing all the major works and developments. Fire elementals are classified as salamanders and exist in campfires, wood, or fire everywhere.

Specifically, Fire corresponds to:

Active, strength, energy, want, vengeance, discomfort, inspiration, radiance, zeal, ambition, violence, limits, commitment, action, imaginative, determination, impulse, motivated, thrilling, courage, bravery, intimidation, fanatic, dissatisfaction...

You have to work with Fire if you want to impact some of these places in your life. Contrary to Water, which has only three colors, Fire has six primary colors:

- Sun Yellow–fire, imagination, lusters.
- Yellow-Orange–Commitment, enthusiasm, operation.
- Red Orange–wind, agony, panic, attack, push.
- Bright-Red–Bravery, bravery, desire, commitment.
- Dark Red–love, wind. Bright Red.
- Electric Blue–Both bands, celestial or fundamental power activation.

Like the Air factor, you can use the Fire element to change various aspects of your life. For example, if you wake up with the "Monday morning blues," try adding Sun Yellow to your setting. For starters, in

Sun Yellow, you might begin dressing, burn a yellow sun candle or place a sun yellow on your pillow.

All these Sun Yellow sources cultivate and feed your soul, boost your spirit's strength, and drive away thoughts of despair and destruction. Sun yellow fill any "void in the soul" feelings you might have (and which you could otherwise seek to fill with food, sleep, or other stunning pleasures). Take it! Give it a try!

More About Salamanders

In his game, Harry Potter played with salamanders, so you can! Salamanders, including wood-burning stoves or campfires, happen around fires. They are ball-shaped, suck up the fire energy, and become visible. In certain areas of the fire, you'll see a ball-shaped cloud, and ashes will spill over them, not on them.

These are useful when increasing wind, keeping the fire colder with less fuel. If you leave an inch of ash at the bottom of the camper, the salamanders will be allowed to linger in the campfire, making re-starting it harder if you return. To bring salamanders about, lay the coals down with dirt, it creates an air insulator from which they can blast. You can catch them later and restart your fire quickly. A flame of a candle sprays tiny sparks called sprites, probably infant salamanders. You should trap them in baby food bottles and hold them there for 30 to 45 seconds. Once you open the jar at that moment, they jump back into the flame of the candle. Have fun! Have fun!

Magical Element Water

The factor Water is the aspect that increases the speed and movement of manifestations. Water is the source of desire, enthusiasm, empathy, action, and expression. To manifest something you have to join the Water Dimension if you want to speed up the manifestation.

Water is related to the west path, the emotional and spiritual direction (since emotions are the "language of the spirit"). Water elementals are called undines or ondines and play in lakes. Water elementals are called indines or ondines. Like sylphs, elemental airs, undines are playful creatures who like to blow up in the water against you.

The Water dimension correlates to Emotions, feelings, insight, affection, Empathy, compassion, intelligence, commitment, desire, ambition, intent, gratitude, honesty, unity, elegance, equilibrium, calmness, fluidity, sorrow, apathy, happiness, love.

You will work with the mystical ingredient Water if you face some life problems in any of these places. The Water Dimension has three key colors, one of which (Water Blue) can be used by all:

- Blue Water – Natural water, hydration, used for diagnosis.
- Deep Blue – Water of mind or feeling.

- Blue-black – Religious water usually connected to "buried unconscious" issues.

Do not use Deep Blue or Blue Black except when you are a trained magician–otherwise, it could create endless depression or regression!

Water can be a very useful tool for solving daily problems. For example, if you have had a really hard day or you have pain in your body, you can actually wash away your pain using the water factor. Just stand in the shower and transfer all your stress, discomfort, terror, and anxiety out to your body and see the water bring everything through the drain. Change the temperature of the water so that it is very neutral, too hot and not too cold. Water contains fire energy, which is the perfect place to get rid of because most discomfort and stresses are the Fire part. This exercise uses the regular flow of water. It may take 2-5 minutes for all excess fire energy to dissipate, so be careful. When you consistently use this practice, you will find that the same levels of discomfort and anxiety are no longer present in your life. In terms of excess firepower, the shower exercise will read literally what is "usual" in your life.

You can use water on a more spiritual level to increase the flow of your manifestations. If you want something to unfold, and it doesn't happen (or doesn't happen fast enough), spend a few minutes every day thinking that the experience is happening now. How would you do if you'd come up with what you wanted? If you can spend some quality time in the optimistic and fun feeling of having already what you want, the realization can come more easily than you can think. Good luck, and have fun! Have fun!

Magical Element Earth

Earth is the physical and final part of the process of manifestation–the part where you want becomes a physical reality. As you can remind yourself of the previous elements, you prepare for the air aspect, jump into the fire element, and apply an immense amount of passion to the water dimension. Your manifestation comes into existence on Earth, and that's not all. The Earth dimension is also related to power, foundations, and longevity. You will need the Earth element if you want to build an empire or succeed in business.

The Planet is connected to the north, where everything is frozen solid. The elementals of the earth are gnomes who dwell in shells. Here's another Earth tidbit–it's always a combination of all the other elements.

Earth, in particular: strength, money, foundation, endurance, structure, the world, the world of being serenity, solidity, boundaries, lands, trade, products, trust, loyalty, persistence, stubbornness, strength, security, anchor, barter, substance, body, base, possessions.

You need to collaborate with Earth if you want to impact any of these places in your life. Planet has three major colors, like the other three magical elements:

- Green grass – vibrant, dynamic Earth living.
- Brown Earth – Stable Earth.
- Black Pure, dead Earth (black holes stuff).

As with other components, Earth colors can be used to change your life's different aspects. For starters, if you're stuck in a rut in your life, check your colors. When you wear more brown shades, you are bound to "catch" things literally, whether you want to or not. The hue of peace and status quo is Earth Red. It also tends to attract and retain the body's overall weight. Ok to get on with it? Try to switch to other colors such as Ocean Blue, Bright Red (which may destroy body fat and add movement), or Sky Blue (that can allow you to see different options and ideas).

Additionally, add some Grass Green to your color scheme when you're primed for more happiness in your life. Grass Green is a vivid, living color that brings to your life a complex appeal— and makes you hold on whatever you like. When money flows like water through your mouth, wear more Green Grass. It will help you to control and sustain your spending habits!

Spotting Gnomes

Gnomes are the most similar to humans to all elementals. Gnomes are also slow and steady since Earth is a slow and solid element. We tend to avoid us because we're much quicker than they are, but if you're patient and move slowly, you can see Gnomes. Look for stone outcroppings with gnomes. Hear taping together like the echo of two bricks, or see a round hole in the cliff that is not there when you look. You don't annoy you, like other elementals, if you don't bother them. They're lonely and grumbling.

Hand Magic and Self Defense

As magicians, it is important to carefully examine the field of self-defense, as we have considerable power and strength. The use of this power and force improperly may cause a widespread reaction. We must be particularly careful to regulate our emotions and not reactively using our skills.

"There is a right to be here and to pursue your own way as long as you don't hinder others from doing the same," according to western magic tradition. This fundamental rule declares our right to live and to follow our own path and, by extension, our right to defend ourselves against those who may seek to prevent us from following our route.

As you rise in magic, you can eventually draw people from various levels who try to interfere with your journey in some way. Writer Clarissa Estes, an author of Women Run with the Wolves, says: "Whoever has beauty in his life knows that it will draw both the shadow and the sun. Don't be surprised. Don't be fooled. Be armed. "Here is a simple thumb rule in self-defense:" When there is an immediate and aggressive personal injury, you have the right to defend yourself by any means, unless you have done anything to facilitate and cause the attack.

Fire bowl

Over the years, almost every spiritual magical and religious scheme on earth has used a fire bowl. While it has been traditionally used to purify places, persons, and artifacts, the fire bowl can be used as a contemplation or divination aid.

Wand

The wall is used as an expression of our own powers as magicians. Contrary to a lot of the popular literature, the Wand is an air instrument and not a fire instrument. Like the devices for the other three items, the wall improves our control because it can allow our hands to hold more air resources. The wall is a great tool to start with as it can't do as much harm as other instruments, like the Athame (magical knife). The Wand helps practitioners to learn other techniques, either by the hand of experienced magicians or by an Athame.

Wizards and shamans use the Wand to connect, heal, and defend. Like Harry Potter films, the Wand is just one of many magical devices that can accommodate air energies only. Throwing lightning bolts or other fire energy through your wall will make it fire.

Athame

Like the other magical items, we use the Athame to increase our own energy and power. The Athame is the sacred instrument of the element of Fire. Many of the wall magical techniques in Harry Potter films can actually be done with Athame, which can accommodate all color bands of fire energy quickly.

The magicians often use the Athame for firebolts, lighting, protection, healing, exile, and self-defense. It is also used to construct sacred space and complete ceremonial cast circles. The Athame should be "keyed" or tailored to your own powers, like other devices, so that you can use it alone.

Chalice

The Chalice is the Water element, and the Water is the Spirit's language, so it can correctly be said that the Chalice is the means of communication with Spirit. Magicians and shamans use the Chalice to scream for devotion, spiritual contact, and regeneration, the formation of sacred space, purification, celebration, rite, and blessing. Known to most, the Chalice also acts for the protection of itself against certain kinds of forces.

Like other magical instruments, the Chalice should be correctly picked and held to its own capacity.

Plate

The Earth Element's Plate is a magical tool that is widely used to build, repair, protect, and defend itself. The cover also referred to as the "pentacle," is a powerful tool that knits and restores broken bones in hours.

The plate is commonly used together with other magical defense and protection instruments, for example, in Tarot readings, divination, or inspection. The plate can also cover and secure mystical devices like Tarot decks and pendulums if not in use.

Divination

The practice of divination is used by fortune tellers, psychics, palmists, spiritual healers, shamans, and magicians. Divination is the method of accessing information that the five senses cannot reach directly.

There are many ways of worship, including direct and indirect worship. The Tarot, the I-Ching, the pendulum, the water bowl, the Chalice, and the Fire cup are some examples of divination. Each of these types of divination is sufficient for various purposes. Others, such as Tarot, are excellent at decrypting complex situations with many causes and pressures (e.g., preventing bills from being voted on in Congress). Others, such as the pendulum, are good for simple and direct responses, for example, whether a certain herb is useful to heal you.

Tarot

The Tarot is an effective and realistic magic instrument for the divinization and spells research and the operation of the Tree of Life. The symbology and concepts underlying the Tarot date back thousands of years. For example, about 600 AD in the Early Christian Church, the priests had small memorandum cards with images on them. The gypsies used similar cards as well. The old Egyptian smart tablets also had images of plates and CDs. These principles are very ancient but are the source of the meaning of modern tarot cards.

As there are so many different cards, sizes, and interpretations of the card out there, it can be hard to know where to start. Starting with the Waite-Rider deck, a plain deck with easy symbols is recommended. The cards are easy to interpret, and the interpretation is less time spent.

We also pointed out that two basic tarot spreads or formats, an easy means to translate cards and the Tarot's fundamental past are all things you need to become a knowledgeable reader. From there, you can connect to other boards, like the Thoth deck.

Sonics

Sonics is a sound study that creates magical effects within us or in the universe around us. Sound of all sorts causes physical, physiological, emotional, and spiritual effects. We're hit by sounds, although we can't hear them, including ultrasonic (sounds too high to pick up our ears) and sub-sonics (sounds too low to listen to our ears).

Navajo curative singers understand the auditory (or sonic) effects and may only use music to treat mental, physical, and emotional problems. Singers are able to use voice, rattles, flutes, and percussion. Our work shows one of the most modern acoustic examples.

Spell work

A spell is a psychical or magical process involving a combination of elements (air, fire, water, and earth) and/or system influences that generate a certain effect over a period of time. A trait could also be characterized as a formalized goal that is implemented over time. We use spells when we cannot influence a situation or circumstance directly, especially when dealing with difficult circumstances or challenges that need a lot of strength to resolve.

Chants, litanies, Sonics, voodoo dolls (simulacra magical), and directors and limiters are all spells in this description. Prayers are charms, too. Spells are energy matrices designed to generate momentum and overcome obstacles until the end goal is achieved. Unless otherwise arranged by administrators and limiters, spells are less immune to the target. Although the purpose may be appropriate in contrast with road rules, the spell route may be highly destructive (and unacceptable in compliance with road rules).

Seven Arrows research reports that when the whole civilized world demanded that Germany be saved from inflationary stagnation after World War I (as it economically pulled everyone down) without explaining what or how these prayers brought Hitler to power. Twice before Hitler tried to take power, but failed both times. At the same time, the Jews fervently hoped that they would return to the Holy Land. At the time, though, the Jewish people were too large to return to the Holy Land safely (they were destroyed by the Arabs)–only a small population was able to return successfully. Jewish priesthood tied into the prayers, which brought Hitler to power, and Hitler's tactics of less opposition diminished the Jews in order to realize the prayers of their return to the Holy Land.

A participant who engaged in a meditation group that taught people how to use white light had similar difficulties. The mediation community encouraged people to place the item on a newsletter board that they needed, to sit there and envision what it was like, and not to hurt them. A hard-working woman wanted to pay for her house and her car and earn a reliable income. She took a photo of her hypothec and signed it "paying." She did the same for the car and pleaded for a free and clear $250.00. Once asked if she was worried about how the presentation would unfold, she responded that she was not. So her boyfriend, who was a very stable person, stopped in the liquor shop one day to buy liquor and bought a gun and killed himself. Life insurance covered the house and car, granting the woman a free and clear payment of $250.00. He was the weakest link in the chain, so the spell worked by him by taking the path of least resistance.

You must be very specific on the use of managers and limiters, simple magical operating rules, and the language used in spell work before you plan or unleash any spell. Note, the world doesn't matter what you are trying to do. Magic is a science of accuracy, and modified methods yield improved outcomes!

TOP TEN TIPS ON HOW TO START THE RIGHT WAY

If you are new to studying magic, visit the public library for books on magic first. Books are one of the best ways to learn tricks. Magic books most often have tricks that you can learn how to use everyday items in the workplace or at home. A lot of magic books can be found for beginners, such as Magic for Dummies and The Complete Idiot's Magic Tricks Guide.

For beginners and babies, there are several basic magical tricks to learn using household items. You should practice interacting with an audience once you have mastered a trick or two.

It can be daunting for a difficult crowd (as a beginner). Choose to demonstrate tricks to nice, appreciative people and offer reviews. It is advised that you focus on a presentation, which is often the answer for your audience.

1. Learn as much as you can about magic

Read and watch

There is some debate about whether reading books on magic or viewing DVDs is easier. I assume that both can be helpful. Of course, much depends on the book or film's content, and the rest depends on your way of studying–whether you learn more quickly by reading or watching or copying at your own speed. Many people use a combination and build large collections of both. Don't worry, though, that you have to buy everything at once. Start with something that attracts you and learn or see, until you buy other things until you have learned the strategies it provides.

Attend lectures

Take every opportunity to see a more experienced presentation by the magician whether you think that you are interested in his / her magic brand or not, and you never know what knowledge nuggets he/she can offer.

Take magic lessons

Reading, watching, and listening are extremely useful, but the fastest and best way to learn is to learn the magical teachings of a really good wizard who is also a very good teacher. I used to run a language school, and after months of trying to teach Spanish, German, Thai, and anything else, we also came to us. You wanted someone to direct you, inspire you, and remind you that you are on the right track. To me, magic is the same. A few lectures at the outset put you into good habits and set the basis for future self-learning. Of course, you can continue taking lessons as long as you like–the more, the better, if you have the right teacher–but it is an excellent investment, especially at the beginning.

2. Practice!

It was previously mentioned, but the secret to magical achievement is enough practice. You should buy a few tricks and perform them in front of the mirror until you can do them without thought. Then you can give an explanation of your mind. If you really train, that separates you from a decent 60 percent of the magicians. Many magicians just want to buy a trick and do it tomorrow.

A pit to which inexperienced magicians through slip is to buy lots of cool tricks and never know them correctly. If you just buy one trick at a time and work on it, you will know what kind of material is perfect for you, not wasting tons.

Don't go for self-jobs, for the simplest tricks, or for a few months or longer when you have done magic. Be rational about what you can do, but also push yourself. You may be surprised at what you can achieve with enough practice (and perhaps some help from a magic teacher).

3. Get to know other magicians

Have a look at your local magic shop (if you have one), enter the local magic society, and find a friend or two. If you're fortunate enough to live next to a magic shop, spend as much time as possible. The dealer can keep you up to date with the magic, and you can meet some fun clients. Many vendors are happy to help and encourage new wizards to teach you tricks that they know you can and like.

Also, joining your local magic club or society is a good idea. There are many of these in the UK, and you should be able to find one within a reasonable distance. Beginners are welcome, and a lot of professional magicians rubbing their hands. In addition to being a forum for gatherings and exchanging ideas with other magicians, a magical society has a calendar of activities with many seminars and contests for you when you are trained.

If you know other magicians, regular meetings with one or two of your fellow magicians can be very useful. You can thus help each other by providing feedback from others on tricks and generally keeping each other motivated and inspired.

Attend conventions

It is always helpful to go to conventions of magic. You will learn the latest tricks, learn from more experienced magicians, and meet some of your heroes with luck.

Keep an eye on the online forums

As a beginner, you might not want to engage in magic politics–indeed, until you find your feet and see a broad picture, at least. Now, I would warn you to be careful to express negative views and to completely avoid rumors. Unfortunately, although there can be great camaraderie among magicians, distressing amounts of mental disgust can also occur.

It can, however, be very informative to join an online forum or two and to see what people are saying. Maybe the biggest is The Magic Café. It is led by Americans, but magicians from all over the world participate in its debates. Magic Bunny is the largest American.

4. Experiment, make existing tricks your own and invent your own tricks

Don't just follow the ' recipe ' slavishly: playthings and see what's happening. It's always cool to invent something. (If you don't know if you've found something new, just inquire, but no-one can take your idea if you have created the original.)

5. Learn about the psychology of magic

There is often no distinction between an all-right magician and a great magician, except appearance. Give the rituals a plot, talk about it, and get the viewer engaged. "Look at this! Look at this! "It's normally not necessary. Why should the public be interested? What draws them?

Do; note that all the campaigns must be inspired from the point of view of the public. When you move the coin from one side to the other, it may be significant, but why does the audience believe you do it? If you have an explanation of it all, it will be much easier for the listener to understand what you are really doing.

6. Work on your presentation skills and confidence

Connecting with the audience is absolutely essential. Call the fans, speak to them (not just in space), get them involved.

It is also important to look comfortable. If you're worried, the audience will feel anxious about you, and your fun will be ruined. I know that it is easy to say and difficult to achieve in the middle of a scary situation, but it is a worth recalling factor. Essentially, as long as you give the illusion you are satisfied, you can get away with a lot. Just as critical as fixing the tricks is that you can joke if something goes wrong.

I cannot stress enough how important public-speaking skills are for the magic to succeed. Being a magician is not only about doing magic; it's about shocking the crowd with an emotional response.

7. Perform for the public as often as possible

The animation of a magician taking a serpent out of a half, which is outstanding and will stand in high regard. The problem is, though, that you may not have expected anything that might go wrong. If you take every opportunity to play before a live audience, from time to time (that is life), you will witness a tragedy, and the next occasion is great. Often things go wrong for everyone; it's important to deal with it smoothly.

If you are anxious about public performance, the only way to overcome it is to do so as often as possible. Force yourself. Pressure yourself. Skill and practice will be better frankly. Don't be turned off if the show goes wrong, but figure out how to change it next time, from your mistakes. Know that you are accountable and have a strong influence on how a show is going. Certainly, there are people who are bad and wouldn't like the world's greatest magician: this is their question, not yours. Feel sorry and carry on.

8. Develop your persona

What separates you from other magicians? Look for and build on your Special Selling Point.

9. Aim to join The Magic Circle as soon as is realistic

As a member of the esteemed magic circle, you have all kinds of benefits. To start with, you will know that you are fine, always encouraging, and that shows us that you are good, so that you don't need to justify. Obviously, it will take a lot of work and preparation to apply –and maybe you won't succeed on your first try–but it's a good target to consider as you begin to take the magic seriously.

10. Enjoy magic and maintain your sense of magic

Once you are cynical and just look at magic as a way of making a living, you are going to lose your edge. Magic is imaginative, relaxing, and it's supposed to be fun! A magic job is hard work, but it also should be a joy.

A BRIEF LOOK AT A FEW COMMON MAGICAL TECHNIQUES—VISUALIZATION, INVOCATION, AND CANDLE MAGIC

What is Visualization?

Visualization is the secret to magic or to psychic ability.

Think of it that way. Your brain controls your body's muscles, and when your brain says,' Go to that side of the room,' you take them automatically based on your brain's intent.

Visualization is much the same. Once you create the visualization, it becomes the "bone" of your spiritual energy effectively. Your spiritual energy is going to "order" this "body."

In "The Key," the popular book (and film) addresses methods in the law of attraction. This explains the creation of a "vision screen" or "dream board," by placing on these board things that you want, representing what you want in your life, and by believing that the world will bring certain things to you.

This helps, but in my humble opinion, it is difficult, because it takes you a lot longer for this to be done because what you do is "upload" yourself with the board pictures to visualize your purpose. Once you have seen something so much (like the towel holder in your kitchen), without much effort, you can quickly see it in your head, so you know what this towel holder has, so you just do not need to worry about the picture of the towel holder!

Don't be selfish about it. Don't be mean. Know that you can create strong visualizations of practice that reflect on your thoughts and that you don't have to have a trick.

It is important to learn how to visualize the image for a certain task while practicing guided visualization strategies using meditation. For starters, you should not try using a can opener if you want to go anywhere. You'd like to use a car, right?

Ok, so it is equally important that you can retain a guided representation of your target or goal without altering the imagery.

How many times have you heard of something like "I should drive to the supermarket, then to the bank and see my mate, and so on." And then the next thing you know, you dream of taking a holiday in Rio! Daydreaming is a crazy, non-self-restricting visualization that does not serve the purpose of attempting to focus spiritual energy towards a certain goal (but daydreaming has a reason, not for the discussion).

You must "imagine" what it means to do with your spiritual energy and "keep" the image with intense focus in your mind. You must be able to look at this mental image and focus on information such as color, shape, inscriptions, or anything that is important for your mission. You must be able to view this three-dimensional vision because this visualized image becomes the source of your divine intent!

Even if it does not suit the intent, simulation should not be limited to photography. If you want to walk around and do something, then visualize that, but don't let your mind get off the job you have scheduled.

The best example of having the vision of a positive idea for a beginner to help put yourself on the right track is the use of a ball (i.e., sphere) of energy and focuses your mind on that ball so it knows what to do when you bring it into the world.

To get started on some basic and sound visualization techniques, see below:

Lesson: Visualization

It is important to "sense" the flow of energy when concentrating on a spiritual energy or psychic power. It assists when visualizing the force behind it.

Via visualization from around, you will create divine forces and canalize the power to achieve your goals. Take the following steps and activities to improve your energy simulation skills. Take your time and work slowly for a short time, as your daily schedule requires. Do not step on until you believe that you have learned the ones in front of it. This is not a sprint, so persistence is necessary for progress.

SEE IT

Find a quiet spot not to be disturbed. Get in a cozy and confident place. Now start to imagine a ball of two colors but forget darker colors like black or red blood. Imagine that the background behind it is a rich neon blue (the color of imagination).

MOVE IT

Now imagine the ball divided in half by the two colors. In your mind, now gently spin and see the two colors you have to change their points of view as the ball spins slowly. As the ball continues to spin on its axis, begin to think about the ball changing directions, up, down, sideways, reverse, etc. You can even have the ball itself move forward and backward from your perception.

CHANGE IT

Finally, after you have felt comfortable watching and moving the ball, move the ball. You can start by combining the colors, making color swirls, rotating the colors, brightening the colors, etc. The lighter and happier the colors, the more positive energy you create. Work on changing the blue background to violet (violet is a greater intuition in nature, while blue reflects a more visual approach).

SEND IT

Think of strength, energy flowing into the disk. Suppose that it radiates with gold or silver, and the light dances as the sun or twinkles like a star. Think of something positive in your life and visualize the demand that goes into the ball and infuses it with even more power. Make sure it does not mess with somebody's life (i.e., seek to get someone to marry you against their will) and use a need instead of a wish. Using green to pay a bill for rent, red to find friendship or love, etc. Now that you're happy for your ball, draw it close to your heart in your chest. Imagine that the ball is moving in. Once she's gone, she's ready to send. Extend your right hand if you're right. Use your left hand if you are left-handed. Think of a divine arm or hand you want to stretch from your chest if you have no wrists. Now give the ball the push (massive speed) from your hands, down the arm, and out the side as you point your head. Imagine the ball going into the sky, your bank account, the sun, the earth, a flower, a bill that should be paid, but note, do not focus on anyone in particular unless you are allowed. Always avoid sending any offensive back. Negativity will come back to you like white on rice and in the midst of a snowstorm like a glass of milk like a paper plate. You don't need that if you try to grow your strength.

Black Box Technique

Imagine the brain's black box. This box is very solid, so dense and impenetrable, that it can't be penetrated from outside even by the smallest pinch. This is a different box because emotions will leave it, but not go back home. The box is so dark that it would not be easy to see if it did not reflect a small amount of visible light from the bottom. Your entire mind and thoughts are in this box now free. There can be nothing in this box, just out. Take the feelings you care about and place them outside the box. You can't pass through the impenetrable black walls that shield your eyes. Have this approach persistently. When you start seeing and distracting yourself, simply pick up where you left off. Place every thought out of the box until the mind inside is calm and ready to think about something else.

Make sure to ignore the black box icon until the work is finished. You can slowly remove it by destroying one wall at a time, or literally visualize it under your will dissolving until it is nothing.

INVOCATION AND THE PROCESS OF MAGIC

Traditional invocation is a method used by magicians to communicate with beings. Invoking means allowing the entity to access your consciousness and control your body partially or fully. Invocation is created for a number of reasons: information: an entity may grant a person access to the details of the entity, but the entity may typically want something in return. Because invocation is the easiest way to provide details, what the individual needs is typically the ability for a while to appreciate the enjoyment of the person's body. The magician must exchange knowledge with the object, allowing it to taste sensations. It will give them information in return so that the magician will have access to it if necessary. This kind of invocation could be seen as a kind of divination, although the magician generally needs very specific information.

POSSESSION

Sometimes an object is invoked to use the body of the invoker. In Wilon, for example, the invoker must curse the load to take over its body completely. That form of ownership is not exclusive to voudoun, but in other customs, you are less likely to meet it. It is very important for the magician to have other people on his side in this kind of ritual, both to keep the body safe and to see what the force is doing, while also capturing whatever details this gives. If the person has it, he or she may move in another language, else he or she will behave like an object. To order to convey the meaning to other individuals, the individual will use the possession to express itself not only in words but in motion and in any other way possible.

HEALING

An individual can be called upon to participate in a healing ritual. If he wants to heal someone, the magician can invoke such a being, and he wants to draw on the tools it can offer to help him cure.

The benefit of summoning a deity is that it can help you direct the healing practice. You can also call an entity if you want to ask it to heal you. This can be beneficial because the company uses its own energies instead of relying on the body's insufficient wealth.

Culture: An object is invoked as a means to worship it in a religious context. The person who calls it does not authorize it to be entirely owned but directs it so that worshippers can communicate with the body. The rite done to call upon the deity is part of the process of worship.

NON-TRADITIONAL INVOCATION

I listed traditional invocation, which means there is and indeed is a non-traditional invocation. I established non-traditional techniques that I explored fully in multimedia magic when I learned that calling is a two-way street. In other words, if I can refer to an object under myself, it can be fair for me to appeal to the individual. Path working, which is a form of therapy where an individual builds a virtual reality, can be used to this end if you interact with an organization. Invocation operates on identity theory. In order to successfully summon an object, the magician needs to identify with the deity and provide a means in which he can reach the magician's body, mind, and spirit. But you can also use the same direction and description to call on the person. It's a case of knowing it enough to enter your consciousness. I considered this kind of invocation more effective for obtaining information from the institution, but it can also be beneficial in a case in which you would like to share essence with the organization. Through having access to the object in its native environment, you can better understand the meaning it presents you with, in exchange for what you owe it.

You can call on a human as well. Since invocation is linked, you can invoke yourself in the individual if you can connect. I called on people to help them unblock or cure themselves. I also have this custom as a way to communicate with others when we make routines at long distances. This kind of call should be made only with the approval of the person to whom you invocate. It is important to remember that you will have access to the emotions, memories of that person, etc., but that person will also have access and may also invoke him/her into you. I think this type of practice is perfect for helping others work on a problem or to synchronize people before doing a magical job.

CANDLE MAGIC

Candle magic is one of the simplest forms of spell casting, and as such, there is no need for an elaborate ritual or ritual equipment. In other words, anyone can cast a spell with a candle. Talk about when you made a wish when you blew the birthday cake off the candles. The same principle applies to candle magic; you just announce your purpose instead of just waiting for your wish to come true.

The birthday candle ritual, if you think about it, is based on three basic mystical principles:

- ✓ Decide on a goal.
- ✓ Visualize the end result.
- ✓ Focus your intent, or will, to manifest that result.

Choosing a Candle

Most magic device practitioners would inform you that the size of your candle is not really significant. Apparently, very large candles can be detrimental. For example, a burning candle that takes three days will deter anyone from the burning of a spell that relies on the burning of the candle.

 short taper candle or a votive candle would usually work well. In some cases, a spell may ask for a certain kind of candles, such as a 7-day candle or a model candle, which is a kind of sympathetic magic. The small menorah candle sold in the kosher section of the grocery shop is one of the most common candles. It is about 4 inches long, white, scentless, and slim. They're great for spell work because of this.

You should always use a brand new spell job candle and not lamps at the dinner table or in the shower the day before. According to some magical traditions, a candle takes vibrations out of the objects around it when it begins to burn. If a used candle is already vibrated, some people think it will lead to a negative or ineffective result.

Candle Colors

When it comes to colors, you may want a range to be appropriate for different magical purposes. Typically, candle magic color correspondences are as follows:

- Red: Courage and health, romantic attraction, and lust.
- Pink: Good love and friendship.
- Orange: Encouragement and appeal.
- Gold: financial gain, business activities, and solar contacts.
- Black: knowledge and security. Gold.
- Green: Financial gain, biodiversity, and vitality.
- Security, patience, and understanding. Light Blue.
- Depression and insecurity in Deep Blue.
- Purple: Ambition and power.
- Brown: plays connected to the environment or object.
- Black: Negative and exile.
- Black: Truth and innocence. Red.
- Silver: Reflection, insight, and celestial interactions.

Remember that it is appropriate to use a white candle instead of any other color in many pagan traditions.

Using Your Candle in Ritual

After a candle, oil, or dress before burning. Before burning. This is a way to establish a psychic connection between you and the fire. In other words, you put your own energies and personal vibrations on the candle and project your intent into the wax before it is burnt.

You need natural oil to dress a candle; often, practitioners prefer grape seed because it does not smell. Unique candle spirit oils from one of the spiritual supply stores are also available. Start at the top of the candle and rub the oil down to the middle. Start at the bottom of the candle and rub the oil in the middle to finish with the first coating of the wax. In certain cultures, the unction is performed the opposite way; start in the middle and work your way to the two ends.

If your job requires herbs to be used, roll the oiled candle in the powdered herbs until they are all covered. Nevertheless, it is important to remember that a candle is only a device. It is not necessarily magical, but a way of creating magic by using the element of fire to transfer one's purpose. Just as other magically intended tools are used, candles should be spiritually cleaned before they are included in a spell.

The basic form of candle magic uses a colorful paper that suits the candle's intent. Decide what your objective is and write it on paper.

In certain rituals, you would write down your target in a magical alphabet such as Theban or Enochian. If you were to spend money, you would write your intentions: "I will be financially successful." Because it's a cash-based work, we'd select a paper of the same color and a bar of gold or green piece. As you enter your goal, you can visualize that goal.

Consider the various ways your aim will manifest, such as through your work. Maybe somebody who owes you money would come out of the blue to pay back the debt. Or perhaps you're going to get a large tax refund check!

After writing down your target, fold the paper, and focus all the time on your intent. Some people like to say a little incantation. It has nothing to fancy. Something that is as plain as:

The extra money comes my way,

I could use a little cash today.

The extra money comes to me,

As I will, so it shall be.

Into the fire of the candle, put one corner of the folding paper, and allow it to catch fire. Hold the paper as long as possible (without burning your fingers) and put it on its own in a fire-safe bowl or in a cauldron. Enable the candle to absolutely flame out. When the candle has burned, replace it instead of saving it for another job. There is generally not much of a candle left but a wax stub, and you can either hide it outside or put it away whatever you want.

Candle Magic for Divination

Candles are used for divinatory purposes in some magical rituals. The two most used ways to worship candles are to decipher the wax and how the candle really flames.

For the holy candle to be lit, you will have to be vigilant whether the candle flames low or high if it flicks or if there is more than one light. Two flames could mean that somebody from the spirit world helps you achieve your goal. Even the colors found in the blaze give you an indication of your spell's efficacy. But there is no consensus on the importance of these signals. While some practitioners believe that a candle that gives tall and strong signs to satisfy their wish, some find out that the duration and consistency of the wick will affect the way the candle burns and the air vent, reflect more on how the candle burns than on your intention.

On the other side, you have to bring the molten wax into a cold water cup if you want to pray by reading the candle wax. The wax hardens and forms almost immediately. Use these ways to answer your questions as much as if you read tea leaves.

Diane J: Lockhart

WITCHCRAFT SPELLS AND RITUALS

What Is A Spell?

The term "spell" is originated from ancient languages, and usually means "to indicate, to explain, to say." In other words, the spell is made up of words (or emojis).

It is usually a word or a sequence of sentences expected to happen. A spell can be used either alone or by actions. It can be used in or by itself in magic ceremonies or in rituals.

You don't have to rhyme spells, and if you want, you can write them yourself. I propose that you use words that don't align with you, rather than someone else.

There's such a quiet spell, with words spoken or written down in someone's memory. The strength of the word is so much greater than thoughts alone, though, that I encourage you to express your gifts, even if you have to whisper them.

What Is A Ritual?

Rituals are more complex works of magic. They usually have some kind of structure, including casting a circle, invoking the quarters/elements, and invoking spirits or gods. They contain ceremonial acts, frequently repeated for other ceremonies, such as the celebration of the full moon.

Rituals are meant to help one travel through the world. These almost always take longer than lessons because they are bigger works of art that collect a great deal of energy. We usually have spells because the magical work is highly complex.

Rituals are more effective in holding and directing the raised energy into an object. Examples of ritual work include spell jars, manifestations/attractions, transformational magic like spiritual regeneration, the magic of protection, and more.

The beauty of everybody looks a bit different. Some people don't ritually name angels or gods, while others like to circle in the simplistic form of magic. It's all up to you how these words are described.

Finally, if you want to say "spell" to your magic practice, that's all right. Only add a couple of words. For instance, "May these tarot cards be encouraged to give me truthful answers to my questions." Incorporating spell work to a rite or activity can only help.

But some writers still propagate this misinterpretation. It's not really a big deal, but I think it's better if you know what it is.

I hope these concepts of spells, practices, and rituals will allow you to express the magical work's complexities!

CONCLUSION

Witchcraft and magic remain vague as terms, nor is current use precisely the same as the earlier definition. Historians have not always received a clear understanding of anthropological analysis concepts in court case content that affect different times and cultures.

The object of witchcraft or magic was-or is supposed to be-injury or cure. Injury by witchcraft in Europe was already an ancient felony in the time of witch persecution. Spell spells have always been used to ensure protection and wealth. Only benevolent magic was commonly considered a crime in Europe of the 16th century or later by secular law. In the past, the learned clergy were more or less persistent in rejecting pagan rites and magic.

The myth-dating back to the 15th century-of witches operating on the Sabbath was special for the European witch-hunts. Although at that time, the idea existed-and still exists in many places today-that the spirit could separate itself from the body and act independently, the hypothesis of the witch coupled with the Devil on a Sabbath by the witches was a particular addition of European civilization to the witchcraft and magic tradition.

Anthropologists have commonly researched witchcraft primarily as a power of bad will or spirit that could harm an opponent or adversary. They understand magic as a process that causes good or evil through various tricks and objects.

The areas were carefully selected for the victims of witchcraft and magic, leading to criminal charges. Two-thirds of the charges against the witchcraft were for injuries, but the victim mostly survived. The next level was livestock abuse (including milk churning and horses). Benevolent magic was usually directed at the healing of people or animals. Fishing, grain-growing, and hunting, for example, were never the target of a criminal charge, whether witchcraft or magic.

Do Not Go Yet; One Last Thing To Do

If you enjoyed this book or found it useful, I'd be very grateful if you'd post a short review on Amazon. Your support does make a difference, and I read all the reviews personally so I can get your feedback and make this book even better.

Thanks again for your support!

Made in the USA
Coppell, TX
30 April 2020